WORDS FROM THE WISE

An arrangement by word and theme of the entire book
Of The Proverbs

By Wesley G. Pippert

Words From The Wise
by Wesley G. Pippert

Printed in the United States of America

ISBN 1-594671-22-2

Xulon Press
www.XulonPress.com

Xulon Press books are available in bookstores everywhere, and on the Web at www.XulonPress.com.

Without counsel purposes are disappointed,
but in the multitude of counsellors they are established
■ Prov. 15:22 (King James Version)

To my "multitude"

The late Wendell Stevens
Don Jones and Mike Ryan
Will Norton and the late Rep. Paul Henry
Scott Cohen, the late Gordon Sabine and Ed Lambeth
Cal Thomas, Ken Daniel and the late Jim Johnson
Andrew Burrows and the late Rick Hurst
Gene Bradley
Ken Bloem and David Zesiger
Gary Anderson

and especially
Craig Barnes

TABLE OF CONTENTS

Introduction

To know wisdom and discipline, understand words of insight, receive discipline in wise dealing, righteousness, justice, and uprightness; that astuteness may be given to the simple-minded, knowledge and discretion to the youth – the wise also may hear and increase in learning, and one of understanding acquire skill, to understand a proverb and a figure, the words of the wise and their riddles. The fear of the lord is the beginning of knowledge; wisdom and discipline stupid ones despise.
— Prov. 1:2-7

The Proverbs is some of the most practical and yet insightful portions of the entire Bible. It tells us what our values ought to be, about our rawest emotions, how to treat our spouses and children, how to relate to friends and neighbors, how much to eat and drink, how to conduct our financial affairs, and about justice and injustice in a sinful world.

Unlike other parts of the Bible, The Proverbs does not deal with the long journey of Israel and the Israelites. Proverbs, although it has a strong emphasis on justice, scarcely mentions caring for the widow, the orphan and the stranger – a concern that occurs again and again in the Law and the Prophets. There are no references to the coming of the Messiah.

Rather, like other parts of the Wisdom Literature, Proverbs is timeless and universal. There also are no historical or geographical references in the book. It is the search for truth in life and all its vicissitudes. It deals with what is right and wrong. What is wise and what is folly? How shall we behave? How shall we relate to others? We learn from them.

Recent critics, such as James Crenshaw (see his <u>Old Testament Wisdom: An Introduction, Revised and Enlarged</u>, Louisville: Westminster John Knox, 1998), have found remarkable similarities between the Wisdom Literature of Israel and that of Egypt and Mesopotamia. They have speculated that in Israel as elsewhere there were professional sages who were responsible for much of the literature.

The text of Proverbs attributes chapters 1-24 to Solomon and chapters 25-29 to King Hezekiah's scribes copied from Solomon. Chapters 30-31 are attributed to persons from a mysterious land of Massa, Agur and King Lemuel, respectively. These latter chapters provide internal evidence to the presence of sages at that time.

My objective is not to examine or ignore the critical scholarship, but rather, using Hebrew, to make a word study by pulling together all identical and related words into categoroies.

Thus, this work:

- Brings together all the verses or parts of a verse in the entire book of the Proverbs that deal with the same issue or topic.
- Captures the nuances of the differing Hebrew words used for a single English word or concept. For instance, there are several Hebrew words for anger, for desire, for fear, for prudence, for poor, etc. Arranging the verses according to each differing Hebrew word allows the reader to draw the subtle distinctions by seeing lumped together all the uses of one Hebrew word.
- Cites, where possible, a biblical figure or example of that word.
- Yet, it is critical to point out that rarely does a word used several times consistently hold to the same precise definition throughout. Thus, a study of this sort, whatever its value, also has a certain downside – that it is impossible, even perilous, to draw hard and fast conclusions.

A few words about the process. I began the arrangement from the English text in the early 1960s. While on assignment in Israel, however, I conceived of arranging the proverbs from the Hebrew in far more detailed form. I used the Masoretic text of the Hebrew Bible as found in The Interlinear Bible (Jay P. Greene Sr., general editor and translator, Grand Rapids: Baker, 1976-1979); and for English definitions, the Compendious Hebrew-English Dictionary (compiled by Reuben Avinoam and revised and edited by M.H. Segal, Tel Aviv: Dvir Publishing), and for modern definitions, The Up-To-Date English-Hebrew Hebrew-English Dictionary (Shimon Zilberman, Jerusalem: Zilberman, 2001). BibleWorks 5, a biblical exegetical software, was invaluable for double-checking my work.

Every verse or portion of a verse was included under every theme suggested in the verse. Thus, many verses recur throughout the book several times. Some of the divisions were arbitrary – for instance – what traits should be included in Chapter XI: Principles, and which should be included under Chapter IV: Godly Traits, or Chapter V: Ungodly Traits?

- All verb and noun forms of the same Hebrew root are lumped together to permit a fuller view of the word. Thus, all occurences of a single word are pulled together. I was somewhat arbitrary in selecting the broader themes – emotions, relationships, justice and politics etc. – to slot the uses of those words.

- Often, where several Hebrew words mean about the same thing, there seems to be a deepening of the meaning, as in the case of anger and sin and poverty, among others. In the case of sin, and here the modern Hebrew provides insight, the meanings seem to worsen from guilt חַטָּאת (hatta'th), to perversity עָוֹן (avvanoth), to wrong פֶּשַׁע (psha), to felony אָשָׁם (ashm). In the case of anger, one can almost sense the deepening progression from indignation כַּעַס (ka'as), to wrath אַף ('af), to rage עֶבְרָה ('evrath), to burning anger חֵמָה (khemah).

There was a similar progression in words generally defined as poor or poverty, from humble עָנִי , ('oni) to needy מַחְסוֹר (makhsov), to destitute אֶבְיוֹן ('evyon)

■ What struck me as well, was the emphasis on justice, for instance in dealing with slavery. Masters are told to pamper their slaves (Prov. 29:21) and not to slander them (Prov. 30:10); on the other hand, slaves are told that if they act wisely they will win the king's favor (Prov. 14:35) and succeed their master (Prov. 29:21).

■ Beside each English definition is the Hebrew word, along with its approximate English pronunication and the modern definition.

■ I also was purposely quite literal in my translations, which represent an amalgam of The Interlinear Bible, the authorized King James version of the Bible, the Revised Standard Version, copyright 1952 by the National Council of Churches, and Young's Literal Translation (1862/1898), drawn from BibleWorks 5. I generally used the same definition of a Hebrew word each time it occurs, with the intention of tying together all instances of the same word. I recognize that occasionally one of the other definitions might better fit a particular verse.

Several things became evident:

■ The sheer number of verses about righteousness and wisdom demonstrate how important these things were to Solomon and the other sages.

■ There are several Hebrew words, for instance, for "poor" and "angry." I separated all the verses using each particular Hebrew word for "poor" and each for "angry." Thus, the reader, by seeing all the ways one particular word was used, can capture the nuance of each word in a much more dramatic way than merely trying to employ modern English verse by verse. The Hebrew language consists only of consonants, with the distinction within a word made by the use of "points." Often the same Hebrew word had completely different meanings, with the distinctions made by the points. Modern Hebrew does not use points, for the most part.

■ I took particular care in dealing with the Hebrew words used for the names of God and for gender distinctions. In accord with most translation, I used God when the Hebrew word was אֱלֹהִים (Elohim) and Lord יהוה (Yahweh). I used the word "man" only when the Hebrew word was אִישׁ (ish), which seemed to imply male. For גְּבַר (gabor) a word meaning warrior often with sexual or military connotation, I used the translation "virile man" or warrior. For אָדָם (adam), a broader word, I used the translation "person." There is only a single instance or two of אֲנָשִׁי (nashee), which I defined as people. I used the pronoun "he" at the start of sentences or phrases only when the Hebrew did; otherwise, I used the neutral "one." I did use "he" on second reference.

■ The Hebrew text is much less sexist than the English translations. Often English versions have inserted "man" where the Hebrew text did not and the pronoun "he" at the start of sentences. For instance, in Prov. 1:1-6 and in 2:21, the word "man" does not occur in the Hebrew.

■ There was evident a certain amount of the structure of parallelism, a characteristic of Hebrew poetry. Recent critics have refined this characteristic – there is parallelism in which the second line is the opposite of the first, there is parallelism in which the second line clarifies the first line; there is parallelism in which the first line builds toward the second. Several times, the writer would make a statement, then, several verses later, make a nearly identical statement, as in the verses on fool. See, for instance, Prov. 16:21 and 23; 19:5 and 9; and 28:6 and 18

In using portions of a verse, I ran the hazard of undermining the theory of the parallelism. To counter this, I used a portion of a verse when it seemed that the portion could stand alone and/or was not directly related to the other portion. If both parts of the verse seemed fused and inseparable, I cited both.

It is not surprising that the modern definitions of the Hebrew word vary little from the biblical uses. The father of modern Hebrew, Eliezer Perlman, a Lithuanian Jew, arrived in Jerusalem in 1882, changed his name to Ben Yahuda and determined to restore to life a language dead for centuries. He succeeded; hence, modern Hebrew, drawn heavily from biblical Hebrew, is little more than a century old. See my <u>Land of Promise Land of Strife: Israel at Forty</u> (Waco: Word, 1988). I found that often the modern Hebrew word blurs some of the distinctions apparent in the biblical word. Yet, occasionally the modern word brings some clarity to the biblical word, as in פָּתַה (patah) in which the biblical translation is deceive or entice and the modern translation is seduce or tempt.

I pay tribute to the late Prof. J. Barton Payne, whose initial assignment was my inspiration for this project; Prof. Andrew Burrows of Hebrew University (and also the godfather of my daughter Elizabeth), who provided invaluable assistance, and Patricia Cloyd, who provided indispensable help at a key moment. Prof. Hassell Bullock, who teaches Wisdom Literature at Wheaton College, read the manuscript and offered suggestions. And always, Elizabeth and David, the lights of my life.

Wesley G. Pippert
Chicago to Jerusalem to Washington

PART I: OURSELVES

Chapter 1: OUR EMOTIONS

Anger

Several Hebrew words are used to indicate deepening degrees of anger. One can almost feel this deepening, beginning as a sort of angry mood, then growing into acts of burning rage.

> indignation, vexation כַּעַס (ka`as) (modern translation – anger)

(The LORD (יהוה Yahweh) was provoked to anger when the people of Israel served other gods, Judges 2:12, and Hannah was provoked when the LORD (יהוה) closed her womb, I Sam. 1:6)

A stupid one is known in the day of his *indignation*,
> Prov. 12:16a

A dullard son is an *indignation* to his father and bitterness to her who bore him.
> Prov. 17:25

Better to dwell in a wilderness land, than with a woman of contentions and *indignation*.
> Prov. 21:19

(From Hezekiah's scribes)
A stone is heavy, and the sand is heavy, and the *indignation* of a fool is heavier than both.
> Prov. 27:3

anger, indignation אַף ('af)

Moses showed this kind of anger upon seeing the Golden Calf, Ex. 32:19, as did Jacob against Rachel when she protested her barrenness, Gen. 30:2, and did David when the prophet Nathan confronted him about the poor man's lamb, II Sam. 12:5

He who is short to *anger* acts foolishly,
— Prov. 14:17a

One who is long (i.e., slow) to *anger* is of great understanding,
but one of short spirit exalts folly.
— Prov. 14:29

A soft answer turns away rage (חֵמָה)
but a harsh word stirs up *anger*.
— Prov. 15:1

A man (אִישׁ ish) of rage (חֵמָה) stirsof rage (חֵמָה),
lest you learn his ways and entangle yourself in a snare.
— Prov. 22:24-25

One who is slow to *anger* is better than the mighty,
and he who rules his spirit than one who takes a city.
— Prov. 16:32

A human being's (אָדָם adam) discretion makes his *anger* slow,
— Prov. 19:11a

A gift in secret subdues *anger*,
and a bribe in the bosom, strong rage (אָדָם).
— Prov. 21:14

Do not associate with a possessor/lord בַּעַל (ba'al) of *anger*,
nor go with a man (אִישׁ ish) of rage (חֵמָה),
lest you learn his ways and entangle yourself in a snare.
— Prov. 22:24-25

26

Note that the Hebrew word for possessor above, is also the name of the Canaanite god Baal.

When your enemy falls do not rejoice,
and when he stumbles do not let your heart be glad;
lest the Lord (יהוה Yahweh) see and it be evil in his eyes,
and turn away his *anger* from him.
—   Prov. 24:17-18

(From King Hezekiah's scribes)
Fierce is rage (חֵמָה) and overflowing is *anger*
but who can stand before jealousy?
—   Prov. 27:4

but the wise turn away *anger*.
—   Prov. 29:8b

A man (אִישׁ ish) of *anger* stirs up contention
and a possessor of rage (אִישׁ) abounds in sin.
—   Prov. 29:22

(From Agur of Massa)
For pressing milk produces curds,
pressing the nose produces blood,
pressing *anger* brings forth strife.
—   Prov. 30:33

<u>wrath, rage</u> עֶבְרָה ('evrah) (modern: anger, fury, wrath)

The Lord cited its constant wrath as one of Edom's four transgressions, Amos 1:11

Wealth does not profit in the day of *wrath*,
—   Prov. 11:4

the hope of the wicked is *wrath*.

— Prov. 11:23b

The king's favor is on a servant who acts wisely
but his *wrath* falls on one who acts shamefully.
— Prov. 14:35

Like a lion's roar is the dread of a king,
one who provokes him to *wrath* sins against his own soul.
— Prov. 20:2

One who sows injustice will reap evil,
and the rod of his *wrath* will fail.
— Prov. 22:8

rage, anger, troubled, sullen זַעַף (tsaf) (modern: anger,
fury)

Joseph found the Egyptians troubled by their dreams, Gen. 40:6

Like a lion's growl is a king's *rage*,
but like dew on the grass is his favor.
— Prov. 19:12

The mouth of a loose woman is a deep pit:
those hated by the Lord (יהוה Yahweh) will fall into it.
— Prov. 22:14

burning anger, wrath, rage חֵמָה (khemah)

Rebecah told Jacob of his brother Esau's rage against him, Gen.
27:44. King Haman was filled with rage when he saw that Mordecai
the Jew was not bowing at his gate, Esther 2:1; likewise, Haman was
filled with rage when he saw Mordecai at the king's gate, Esther 5:9.

For jealous (is) the virile man (גֶּבֶר gabor) of *rage*,
and he will not spare in the day of vengeance.

28

— Prov. 6:34

A soft answer turns away *rage,*
but a harsh word stirs up anger (אַף.) (`af)
— Prov. 15:1

A man (אִישׁ ish) of *rage* stirs up strife,
but he who is long (i.e., slow) to anger (אַף.)calms fighting.
— Prov. 15:18

A king's *rage* is a messenger of death,
and a wise man will cover it.
— Prov. 16:14

One of *rage* will bear the penalty,
for if you deliver him you will only have to do it again.
— Prov. 19:19

A gift in secret subdues anger (אַף,)
and a bribe in the bosom, strong *rage.*
— Prov. 21:14

Do not associate with a possessor of anger (אַף,)
nor go with a man (אִישׁ ish) of burning anger,
lest you learn his ways and entangle yourself in a snare.
— Prov. 22:24-25

(From King Hezekiah's scribes)
Cruel is *rage* and overflowing is anger (אַף)

but who can stand before jealousy?
— Prov. 27:4

A man (אִישׁ ish) of anger (אַף) stirs up contention
and a possessor of *rage* abounds in sin.
— Prov. 29:22

Anxiety, worry דְּאָנָה (dagah) (modern: anxiety, care, concern, worry)

The Lord (יְהוָה Yahweh) concerning Damascus, "they are troubled like the sea," Jeremiah 49:23

Anxiety in a man's (אִישׁ ish) heart weighs him down.
— Prov. 12:25a

Bitterness מָרָה (marah) (modern: embitter, distress) and מֶמֶר (memer)

Esau's family made life bitter for Isaac and Rebekah, Gen. 26:35. Hannah wept bitterly over her barrenness, I Sam. 1:10.

The heart knows its soul of *bitterness,*
— Prov. 14:10a

A dull son is a grief to his father
and *bitterness* to her who bore him.
— Prov. 17:25

Jealousy and desire

The Hebrew words demonstrate the close relationship between jealousy and desire.

lust, passion תַּאֲוָה (ta`avah) (modern: lust, passion)

After the Fall, the Lord God אֱלֹהִים יְהוָה Yahweh Elohim) told Eve her passion would be toward her husband, Gen. 3:16, and a short time later, the Lord (יְהוָה) told Cain that sin's passion was aimed at him, Gen. 4:7.

What the wicked fears shall come upon him
but the *passion* of the righteous is given.
— Prov. 10:24

The *passion* of the righteous is only good,
the hope of the wicked is wrath.
— Prov. 11:23

Hope deferred makes the heart sick,
but a *passion* fulfilled is a tree of life.
— Prov. 13:12

A *passion* fulfilled is sweet to the soul,
— Prov. 13:19a

Through *passion* he who has separated himself
seeks and breaks out against all sound wisdom.
— Prov. 18:1

The *passion* of a human being (אָדָם adam) is his mercy,
and it is better to be poor than a man (אִישׁ ish) of a lie.
— Prov. 19:22

The *lust* of the lazy one kills him
for his hands refuse to labor.
All day long he *lusts* with *lust,*
but the righteous gives and withholds not.
— Prov. 21:25-26

Do not eat the bread of an evil eye
and do not *desire* his delicacies.
— Prov. 23:6

Do not envy men (אִישׁ ish) of evil,
and do not have a *passion* to be with them.
— Prov. 24:1

  desire, lust (חֵפֶץ) (khefets) (modern: desire, want, wish)

31

Hamor and son Shechem desired Jacob's daughter Dinah, Gen. 34:19

all your *desires* are not likened to her (wisdom).
—   Prov. 3:15

desire, lust, mischief (הַוֹּת) (hawath)

> *The Hebrew word is very similar to that of ruin, calamity*

The Lord (יהוה Yahweh) does not allow the soul of the righteous to go hungry,
But he pushes away the the wicked's *desire*.
—   Prov. 10:3

An evil-doer listens to evil lips,
and a liar gives heed to a tongue of evil *desire*.
—   Prov. 17:4

envy, jealousy קִנְאָה   (qin`ah) (modern: jealousy, envy)

> *The Lord says that if a man is jealous and suspicious of his wife, he shall take her to a priest, Num. 5:11ff.*

Be not *envious* of a man (אִישׁ ish) of violence,
nor fix thou on any of his ways.
—   Prov. 3:31

For *jealous* (is) the virile man (גֶּבֶר gabor) of burning anger,
and he will not spare in the day of vengeance.
—   Prov. 6:34

but *jealousy* is the rottenness of bones.
—   Prov. 14:30b

Let not your heart *envy* sinners,

but continue in the fear of the Lord (יהוה Yahweh) all the day.
— Prov. 23:17

Do not *envy* men (אִישׁ ish) of evil,
and do not have a passion to be with them.
— Prov. 24:1a

and be not *envious* of the wicked ...
the lamp of the wicked will be put out.
— Prov. 24:19b, 20b

(From Hezekiah's scribes)
Fierce is fury and overflowing is anger
but who can stand before *jealousy?*
— Prov. 27:4

desire, delight חָמַד (khemed) (modern: covet, desire)

(From King Hezekiah's scribes)
Fierce is fury and overflowing is anger
but who can stand before *jealousy?*
— Prov. 27:4

The Lord God causes to sprout from the ground every tree desirable for appearance, and good for food, and the tree of life in the midst of the garden, and the tree of knowledge of good and evil, Gen. 2:9.

A treasure to be *desired*, and oil, is in the habitation of the wise,
And a foolish human being (אָדָם adam) swalloweth it up.
— Prov. 21:20

Grief, sadness תּוּגָה (tugah) (modern: sorrow, grief)

The psalmist says his soul has melted from sorrow and he asks to be strengthened by the word, Psalms 119:28

a dull son is the *grief* of his mother.
—　Prov. 10:1

Even in laughter is the heart pained,
And the latter end of joy *is sadness.*
—　Prov. 14:13

The father of a dullard *grieves* over it,
—　Prov. 17:21a

Happy, blessed אַשְׁרֵי (`ashre) (29)

*Leah said she was happy when her maid Zilpah bore her husband
Jacob a son Asher, Gen. 30:13. The Queen of Sheba told Solomon
his servants were happy, I Kings 10:8.*

And now, my sons, listen to me;
happy are those who keep my ways.
Hear instruction and be wise, and do not neglect it.
Happy is the human being (אָדָם) who listens to me,
watching daily at my gates, waiting beside my doors.
For he who finds me finds life and obtains favor from the Lord;
but he who misses me injures himself;
all who hate me love death."
—　Prov. 8:32-36

but *happy* is he who favors the poor.
—　Prov. 14:21b

and he who trusts in the Lord (יהוה Yahweh) is *happy.*
—　Prov. 16:20b

The righteous walks about in his integrity—
happy are his sons after him.
—　Prov. 20:7

(From King Lemuel of Massa)

Her children rise up and call her *blessed.*
—   Prov. 31:28

Healing רְפֻאוֹת (rif uth) (modern: cure, heal)

The people of Judah mocked the messengers of God (הָאֱלֹהִים
Elohim) despised His words and scoffed at His prophets until the
wrath of the LORD (יְהוָה Yahweh) was aroused until there was no
healing, II Chron. 36:16. Lord says there is no healing for Egypt,
Jer. 12:11)

Be not wise in your eyes;
fear the Lord (היה Yahweh) and turn away from evil.
It will be *healing* to your navel and moisture to your bones.
—   Prov. 3:7-8

My son, be attentive to my words;
incline your ear to my sayings.
Let them not escape from your sight;
keep them in your heart.
For they are life to him who finds them,
and *healing* to all his flesh.
—   Prov. 4:20-22

A worthless person, an evil man, goes about with crooked speech,
winks with his eyes, scrapes with his feet, points with his finger,
with perverted heart devises evil, continually sowing discord,
therefore calamity will come upon him suddenly;
in a moment he will be broken beyond *healing.*
—   Prov. 6:12-15

but the tongue of the wise brings *healing.*
—   Prov. 12:18b

but a faithful ambassador is *healing.*
—   Prov. 13:17b

A heart of flesh is *healing* to life,
—   Prov. 14:30a

A *healing* tongue is a tree of life,
—   Prov. 15:4a

Pleasant words flowing with honey are sweetness to the soul,
and *healing* to the bones.
—   Prov. 16:24

A joyful heart makes good *healing*,
—   Prov. 17:22a

(From King Hezekiah's scribes)
He who is often reproved, yet stiffens his neck
will suddenly be broken beyond *healing*.
—   Prov. 29:1

Hope תּוֹחֶלֶת (tokheleth) (modern: expectation, hope)

Naomi talked to her widowed daughters-in-law about the hope of a husband, Ruth 1:12.

The *hope* of the righteous ends in gladness
—   Prov. 10: 28a

In the death of a wicked human being (אָדָם adam) *hope* shall
perish
—   Prov. 11:7a

the *hope* of the wicked is wrath.
—   Prov. 11:23

Hope deferred makes the heart sick,
—   Prov. 13:12a

Discipline your son while there is *hope*
—   Prov. 19:18a

Surely there is a future and your *hope* will not be cut off.
—   Prov. 23:18

So knowledge of wisdom shall be to your soul;
when you find there is a future,
and your *hope* is not be cut off.
—   Prov. 24:14

Do you see a man (אִישׁ ish) wise in his own eyes?
There is more *hope* for a fool than for him.
—   Prov. 26:12

Do you see a man (אִישׁ ish) hasty in his words?
There is more *hope* for a fool than for him.
—   Prov. 29:20

Joy (שִׂמְחָה) (simkhah) (modern: joy, happiness, celebration, festivity)

The women of Israel sang songs of joy after David killed the Philistine Goliath, I Sam. 18:6.)

The hope of the righteous is *joy*,
—   Prov. 10:28

but to the counselors of peace is *joy*.
—   Prov. 12:20b

The light of the righteous *rejoices,*
—   Prov. 13:9a

and its (the heart's) *joy* a stranger does not share.
—   Prov. 14:10b

and the end of *joy* is grief.
— Prov. 14:13b

A *joyful* heart makes a good face,
— Prov. 15:13a

Folly is *joy* to him who lacks heart,
— Prov. 15:21a

A man (אִישׁ ish) has *joy* by the answer of his mouth,
and a word in its time, how good!
— Prov. 15:23a

The light of the eyes *rejoices* the heart,
— Prov. 15:30a

and the father of a fool will not *rejoice* over it.
— Prov. 17:21b

When justice is done, it is a *joy* to the righteous
— Prov. 21:15a

A man (אִישׁ ish) who loves *joy* will be poor,
— Prov. 21:17a

If your heart is wise,
even my heart shall *rejoice.*
— Prov. 23:15

When your enemy falls, do not *rejoice*
— Prov. 24:17

(From King Hezekiah's scribes)
Oil and perfume give *joy* to the heart,
— Prov. 27:9a

Be wise, my son, and give joy to my heart,

that I may answer him who reproaches me.
— Prov. 27:11

When the righteous increase, the righteous *rejoice*,
— Prov. 29:2a

A man (אִישׁ ish) who loves wisdom *rejoiceth* his father,
— Prov. 29:3a

but the righteous sing and *rejoice*.
— Prov. 29:6b

Laugh, make merry (שָׂחַק) (sakhaq)

Job said he was a laughingstock to his friends, Job 12:4

I was at his side, a workman, and I was His delights,
day by day *making merry* before him at every time,
making merry in the world, His land,
and my delights were with the sons of human beings (אָדָם adam).
— Prov. 8:30-31 *(Wisdom is speaking)*

Love and hate

Love and hate, like so many things, are morally neutral. It depends on how each is used. The Wisdom Literature makes this clear.

For he who finds me finds life and obtains favor from the Lord
(יהוה Yahweh)
but he who misses me injures himself;
all who *hate* me *love* death.
— Prov. 8:35-36. *(Wisdom is speaking.)*

Do not reprove a scoffer, or he will *hate* you;
correct a wise man, and he will *love* you.
— Prov. 9:8a

Hatred stirs up contention,
but *love* covers all sins.
—   Prov. 10:12

He who spares the rod *hates* his son,
but he who *loves* him disciplines him.
—   Prov. 13:24

Even the poor is *hated* by his neighbor,
but the *lovers* of the rich are many.
—   Prov. 14:20

Better is a dinner of herbs where *love* is,
than a fatted ox and *hatred* with it.
—   Prov. 15:17

love   אהב (`ahav) (modern: like, love)

Love can be wrong. See Prov. 17:19 and 21:17

Until when, simple ones, will you *love* simplicity,
—   Prov. 1:22

love her (wisdom) and she will guard you.
—   Prov. 4:6b

She (wisdom) is a *loving* deer and a graceful doe,
—   Prov. 5:19a

Come let us drink our fill of *love* until morning,
let us solace ourselves with *love*.
—   Prov. 7:18 (the whore is speaking)

I *love* those who *love* me,
and those who seek me diligently find me.
—   Prov. 8:17 (Wisdom is speaking.)

I walk in the way of righteousness in the paths of justice,
to cause my *lovers* to inherit wealth
and I will fill their warehouses.
—   Prov. 8:20-21

correct a wise man, and he will *love* you.
—   Prov. 9:8b

but the Lord (יהוה Yahweh) *loves* him who pursues righteousness.
—   Prov. 15:9b

he who speaks uprightly is *loved.*
—   Prov. 16:13

He who covers (i.e. forgives) sin seeks *love,*
—   Prov. 17:9a

He who *loves* transgression loves strife,
—   Prov. 17:19a

Life and death are in the hand of the tongue,
and those *loving* it shall eat its fruit.
—   Prov. 18:21

He who gets heart *loves* his own soul,
he who keeps understanding finds good.
—   Prov. 19:8

Do not *love* sleep, lest you become poor.
—   Prov. 20:13a

A man (איש ish) who *loves* joy will be poor,
he who *loves* wine and oil will not be rich.
—   Prov. 21:17

(From King Hezekiah's scribes)

Better is revealed correction than concealed *love*.
Faithful are the wounds of a *lover*,
profuse are the kisses of an enemy.
— Prov. 27:5-6

hate שָׂנֵא (sane`) (modern: hate, dislike)

*Note similarity to שׂוֹנֵא ,enemy. Jacob hated Leah, Gen. 29:31,
and Joseph's brothers hated him, Gen. 37:5 Not all hate is bad.
See Prov. 8:13, 15:27, 28:16*

For they *hated* knowledge
and chose not the fear of the Lord (יהוה Yahweh)
— Prov. 1:29

and you say, "How I *hated* discipline!"
— Prov. 5:12

Six things the Lord (יהוה Yahweh) *hates,*
— Prov. 6:16

The fear of the Lord is *hatred* (יהוה Yahweh) of evil.
Pride and arrogance and the way of evil and perverted speech I
hate.
— Prov. 8:13

He who conceals *hatred* has lying lips,
and one sending out slander is a fool.
— Prov. 10:18

One suffers evil when he is surety for a stranger,
but one *hating* strikers is safe.
— Prov. 11:15

A word of falsehood *hates* the righteous,
— Prov. 13:5a

but one *hating* correction is boorish.
—   Prov. 12:1b

He who is short to anger acts foolishly,
and the plot of a man (אִישׁ) is *hatred*.
—   Prov. 14:17a

Even of his neighbour is the poor *hated,*
—   Prov. 14:20

Better a meal of herbs and love
than being stalled with an oxen and *hatred* with it.
—   Prov. 15:17

and the one *hating* correction shall die.
—   Prov. 15:10b

but one who *hates* bribes shall live.
—   Prov. 15:27

All the brothers of a poor one *hate* him,
—   Prov. 19:7a

(From King Hezekiah's scribes)
make your foot scarce at your neighbor's house
lest he be full of you and *hate* you.
—   Prov. 25:17

If he who *hates* you is hungry, cause him to eat bread,
 And if he thirst, cause him to drink water.
—   Prov. 25:21-22

Hatred is covered by guile,
—   Prov. 26:26

He who *hates*, dissembles with his lips
and harbors deceit in his heart;

though his *hatred* be covered with guile,
his wickedness will be exposed in the assembly.
—   Prov. 26:24-26

A lying tongue *hates* those it crushes,
and a flattering mouth works ruin.
—   Prov. 26:28

Faithful are the wounds of a lover,
profuse are the kisses of a *hated* one.
—   Prov. 27:6

(A ruler) *hating* unjust gain prolongs his days.
—   Prov. 28:16

Humanity אַנְשֵׁי (`nashee) of blood *hate* the upright,
—   Prov. 29:10a

He who shares with a thief *hates* his soul;
he hears an oath but does not tell it.
—   Prov. 29:24

(From Agur of Massa)
Under three things the earth trembles;
under four it cannot bear up:
when a servant reigns, and when a fool is filled with food;
and a *hated* one (woman) is married,
and when a maid becomes heir to her mistress.
—   Prov. 30:21-23

Panic, dread פַּחַד (pakhad) (modern: fear, fright, awe)

He who dwells in the shelter of the Almighty .... shall not fear the dread of the night, Psalms 91:1a, 5a

And whoso is hearkening to me dwelleth confidently,

And is quiet from *dread* of evil!'
— Prov. 1:33

Do not be afraid of sudden *panic*
or of the ruin of the wicked, when it comes;
for the Lord will be your confidence
and will keep your foot from being caught.
— Prov. 3:25-26

(From King Hezekiah's scribes)
O the happiness of a person *fearing* (God, implied) continually
— Prov. 28:14

Separation

An evil man seeketh only rebellion,
And a fierce messenger is sent against him.
— Prov. 17:11

He who separates himself (is estranged)
seeks desire to break out against all practical wisdom.
— Prov. 18:1

Shame

shame, ignominy, disgrace קָלוֹן (qalon) (modern: dishonor,
shame)

The psalmist prays that his enemies would be put to shame, Psalms 83:17

The wise will inherit honor,
but fools get *disgrace*.
— Prov. 3:35

He who committeth adultery *with* a woman lacketh heart,
He is destroying his soul who doth it.

45

A stroke and *disgrace* he doth find,
And his reproach is not wiped away,
—   Prov. 6:32-33

One rebuking a scorner takes *disgrace* for himself,
—   Prov. 9:7a

Comes pride, then comes *disgrace*.
—   Prov. 11:2a

an astute one covers *disgrace*.
—   Prov. 12:16

Poverty and *disgrace* come to one who ignores discipline,
—   Prov. 13:18

and with *disgrace* comes reproach.
—   Prov. 18:3

(From King Hezekiah's scribes)
Do not go out to fight hastily,
lest what you shall do in the end of it,
your neighbor has shamed you.
Debate thy cause with your neighbor...
Lest he who hears your report and returns not puts you to shame.
—   Prov. 25:8-10a

    causing shame   מֵבִישׁ (mevish) (modern: disgraceful, shameful)

The King of Assyria returned home in shame after his raid on Jerusalem and King Hezekiah failed, II Chron. 32:20

he who sleeps in harvest is a son *causing shame*.
—   Prov. 10:5b

Righteousness exalts a nation

but a shame to the people is sin.
A servant who deals wisely has the king's favor,
but his wrath falls on one *causing shame*.
— Prov. 14:34-35

A servant who acts skillfully
shall rule over a son who *causes shame*,
— Prov. 17:2a

He who chases away his father and his mother
is a son *causing shame* and bringing reproach.
— Prov. 19:26

a child left to himself *causes shame* to his mother.
— Prov. 29:15b

Spirit רוּחַ (ruakh) (modern: wind, air, spirit, mind, soul, ghost)

This is the same word that is used in the Hebrew Bible for the Spirit of God (אֱלֹהִים Elohim), as the one active in Creation in Gen. 1. But it is seldom used in Proverbs to refer to the Spirit of God.)

Turn back at my warning, behold, I will pour out to you my *spirit*,
— Prov. 1:23

One carrying slander is a revealer of secrets,
but one of a faithful *spirit* covers the matter.
— Prov. 11:13

Whoso is troubling his own house inheriteth *wind*,
— Prov. 11:29

but one short of *spirit* (i.e., temper) exalts folly.
— Prov. 14:29

but perversity in (the tongue) breaks the *spirit.*
—   Prov. 15:4b

but by the pain of heart the *spirit* is stricken.
—   Prov. 15:13a

All the ways of a man are pure in his own eyes,
but the Lord weighs the *spirit.*
—   Prov. 16:2

Pride goes before destruction,
and before stumbling, a haughty *spirit.*
Better is lowness of spirit with the poor,
than to divide the spoil with the proud.
—   Prov. 16:18-19

and he who rules his *spirit* (is better) than he who takes a city.
—   Prov. 16:32

a stricken *spirit* dries up the bones.
—   Prov. 17:22b

and he who has a cool *spirit* is a man (ish) of understanding.
—   Prov. 17:27b

The spirit of a man (ish) will endure his sickness,
but a broken *spirit* who can bear?
—   Prov. 18:14

(From King Hezekiah's scribes)
Like a broken down city without a wall
is a man (אִישׁ ish) who cannot control his *spirit.*
—   Prov. 25:28

The pride of a man brings him low,
but the humble of *spirit* takes hold of honor.
—   Prov. 29:23

Chapter 2: OUR RELATIONSHIPS

FAMILY בַּיִת (bayit)

The word בַּיִת actually means house, and it appears frequently in Proverbs with this meaning. The word also suggests household or family, and in the following verses this is the context.

He who troubles his *house* will inherit the wind,
—   Prov. 11:29a

He who is greedy of gain troubles his *house*,
—   Prov. 15:27a

He who returns evil for good,
evil will not depart from his *house*.
—   Prov. 17:13

(From King Hezekiah's scribes)
Like a bird that strays from its nest,
is a man (אִישׁ ish) who strays from his place.
—   Prov. 27:8

wife אִשָּׁה (`ishshah)

The same Hebrew word is used for both woman and wife. The context determines which.
The following verses indicate "wife."

...and rejoice in the *wife* of your youth,
a lovely hind, a graceful doe.

Let her affection fill you at all times,
be infatuated always with her love.
—   Prov. 5:18b-19

A good *wife* is the crown of her husband,
and she who brings shame is like rottenness in his bones.
—   Prov. 12:4

He who finds a *wife* finds a good thing,
and obtains favor from the Lord (יהוה   Yahweh)
—   Prov. 18:22

and a continual dripping (of rain) is a contentious *wife*
....
but a prudent *wife* is from the Lord יהוה(Yahweh)
—   Prov. 19:13b-14b

It is better to live in a corner of the housetop
than in a house with a contentious *wife*.
—   Prov. 21:9, 25:24

It is better to live in a land of wilderness
than with a contentious and fretful *wife*.
—   Prov. 21:19

(From King Hezekiah's scribes)
A continual dripping on a rainy day
and a contentious *wife a*re alike;
to restrain her is to restrain the wind
or to grasp oil in his right hand.
—   Prov. 27:15-16

(From King Lemuel of Massa)
A good *wife* who can find?
She is far more precious than jewels.
The heart of her husband trusts in her,
and he will have no lack of gain.

She does him good, and not harm,
all the days of her life.
She seeks wool and flax,
and works with willing hands.
She is like the ships of the merchant,
and she brings food from afar.
She arises while it is yet night
and provides food for her household and tasks for her
handmaidens.
She considers a field and buys it;
with the fruit of her hands she plants a vineyard.
She girds her loins with strength and makes her arms strong.
She perceives that her merchandise is profitable.
Her lamp does not go out at night.
She puts her hand to the poor,
and reaches out her hands to the destitute.
She is not afraid of snow for her household,
for all her household are clothed in scarlet.
She makes herself coverings;
her clothing is fine linen and purple.
Her husband is known in the gates,
where he sits among the elders of the land.
She makes linen garments and sells them;
she delivers girdles to the merchant.
Strength and dignity are her clothing,
and she laughs at the time to come.
She opens her mouth with wisdom,
and the teaching of mercy is on her tongue.
She looks well to the ways of the household,
and does not eat the bread of idleness.
Her children rise up and call her blessed;
her husband also, and he praises her.
Many women have done excellently,
but you surpass them all.
Charm is deceitful, and beauty is vain,
but a woman who fears the Lord (יהוה Yahweh) is to be praised.
Give her of the fruit of her hands,

and let her works praise her in the gates.
—   Prov. 31:10-31

<u>both parents</u>

Heed, my son, your father's discipline,
and reject not your mother's law;
for they are a fair garland for your head,
and pendants for your neck.
—   Prov. 1:8-9

My son, keep your father's commandment,
and forsake not your mother's law.
Bind them upon your heart always;
tie them about your neck.
When you walk, they will lead you;
when you lie down, they will watch over you;
and when you awake, they will talk with you.
For the commandment is a lamp and the teaching a light,
and the reproofs of discipline are the way of life,
to preserve you from the evil woman,
from the smooth tongue of the adventuress.
—   Prov. 6:20-24

A wise son makes a father rejoice
and a dull son is a grief to his mother.
—   Prov. 10:1

He who curses his father or is mother ,
His lamp will be put out in blackest darkness.
—   Prov. 20:20

Hearken to your father who begot you,
and do not despise your mother when she is old.
—   Prov. 23:22

The father of the righteous will greatly rejoice;
he who begats a wise son will be glad in him.
Let your father and mother be glad,
let her who bore you rejoice.
—   Prov. 23:24-25

(From King Hezekiah's scribes)
He who robs his father or his mother and says,
"That is no transgression,"
is the partner to a man who destroys.
—   Prov. 28:24

(From Agur of Massa)
There are those who curse their fathers
and do not bless their mothers.
There are those who are pure in their own eyes
but are not cleansed of their filth.
There are those – how lofty are their eyes,
how high their eyelids lift!
There are those whose teeth are swords, whose teeth are knives,
to devour the poor from off the earth,
the needy from among men.
—   Prov. 30:11-14

The eye that mocks a father and scorns to obey a mother
will be picked out by the ravens of the valley
and eaten by the vultures.
—   Prov. 30:17

father אָב ('av)

See also references to father above in the verses about parents

for the Lord (יהוה Yahweh) reproves him who he loves,
as a *father* the son in whom he delights.
—   Prov. 3:12

Heed, O sons, a *father*'s discipline,
and be attentive, that you may obtain understanding;
for I give you good precepts:
do not forsake my teaching.
When I was a son with my father, tender,
the only one in the sight of my mother,
he taught me, and said to me,
"Let your heart hold fast my words,
and keep my commandments, and live;
do not forget, and do not turn away from the words of my mouth.
Get wisdom, get understanding.
Do not forsake her, and she will keep you;
love her, and she will guard you.
The beginning of wisdom is this:
Get wisdom, and whatever you get, get understanding.
Prize her highly, and she will exalt you;
she will honor if you embrace her;
she will bestow on you a beautiful crown."
—   Prov. 4:1-9

A wise son hears his *father*"s instruction
But a scoffer does not hear rebuke.
—   Prov. 13:1

A fool despises his *father's* instruction,
But one keeping correction is astute.
—   Prov. 15:5

The crown of old men is the children of children (i.e., grandchildren),
and the glory of children is their *fathers*.
—   Prov. 17:6

Ruin to his *father* is a foolish son,
—   Prov. 19:13

Do not move the old landmark your *fathers* have set.
— Prov. 22:28

(From King Hezekiah's scribes)
He who keeps the law is a wise son
but the friend of gluttons shames his *father*.
— Prov. 28:7

A man אִישׁ (ish) who loves wisdom makes his *father* glad,
but a friend of whores wastes wealth.
— Prov. 29:3

mother אֵם (`em)

See parents section above

(From King Hezekiah's scribes)
The rod and reproof give wisdom
but a child left to himself brings shame to his *mother*.
— Prov. 29:15

children בָּנִים (banim) בֵּן (son = ben)

And I do see among the simple ones, I discern among the *children*,
 A youth נַעַר (nyr) lacking heart (also, courage or moral character).
— Prov. 7:7

A wise *son* makes a father rejoice
and a dull *son* is a grief to his mother.
— Prov. 10:1

A *son* who gathers in summer is wise,
but a *son* who sleeps in harvest brings shame.
— Prov. 10:5

A wise *son* heeds his father's discipline.
—   Prov. 13:1

He who spares the rod hates his *son*,
but he who loves him disciplines him.
—   Prov. 13:24

In the fear of the Lord (יהוה Yahweh) one has strong confidence,
and to his *children* shall be a hiding place.
—   Prov. 14:26a

A wise *son* makes a glad father,
but a foolish person אָדָם despises his mother.
—   Prov. 15:20a

A servant who acts wisely will rule over a *son* who acts
shamefully,
and will share the inheritance as one of the brothers.
—   Prov. 17:2

The crown of old men is the children of children (i.e.,
grandchildren),
and the glory of *children* is their fathers.
—   Prov. 17:6

A foolish *son* is a grief to his father
and bitterness to her who bore him.
—   Prov. 17:25

A foolish *son* is ruin to his father,
—   Prov. 19:13a

Discipline your *son* while there is hope,
do not set your heart on his destruction.
—   Prov. 19:18

The *son* who assaults his father and chases away his mother
causes shame and brings reproach.
—   Prov. 19:26

Cease, my *son*, to hear discipline
only to stray from words of knowledge.
—   Prov. 19:27

The righteous walks about in his integrity—
blessed are his *children* after him.
—   Prov. 20:7

(From King Hezekiah's scribes)
Be wise, my *son*, and give joy to my heart,
that I may answer him who reproaches me.
—   Prov. 27:11

He who keeps the law is a wise *son.*
—   Prov. 28:7

Discipline your *son*, and it will get you rest;
and it will give delight to your soul.
—   Prov. 29:17

(From King Lemuel of Massa)
Her (a good wife's) *children* rise up and call her blessed;
—   Prov. 31:28a

      youths, boys נַעַר (na'ar)   (modern: boy, lad, youth)

And I do see among the simple ones, I discern among the children,
 A youth lacking heart (also, courage or moral character).
—   Prov. 7:7

Even a *youth* makes himself known by his acts,
whether what does is clean and upright.
—   Prov. 20:11

If one curses his father or his mother,
his lamp will be put out in utter darkness.
—   Prov. 20:20

Train up a *youth* in the way he should go,
and when he is old he will not depart from it.
—   Prov. 22:6

Folly is bound up in the heart of a *youth*,
but the rod of discipline drivs it far from him.
—   Prov. 22:15

Do not withhold discipline from a *youth*;
if you beat him with a rod, he will not die.
If you beat him with the rod, you will save his life from Sheol.
—   Prov. 23:13-14

(From King Hezekiah's scribes)
The rod and reproof give wisdom
but a *youth* left to himself brings shame to his mother.
—   Prov. 29:15

grandchildren

A good (person, implied) leaves an inheritance to the children of
his children,
—   Prov. 13:22a

Sons of sons are the crown of the aged,
and the glory of children is their fathers.
—   Prov. 17:6

brother אָח (`akh)

There are six things which the Lord (יהוה Yahweh) hates, seven
which are an abomination to him ... a man who sows discord
among *brothers*.
— Prov. 6:16, 19b

and a *brother* is born for adversity.
— Prov. 17:17b

A *brother* offended is like a strong city (in terms of being won)
— Prov. 18:19a

A man's אִישׁ (ish) friends may be broken up
but there is one who sticks closer than a *brother*.
— Prov. 18:24

All the *brothers* of a poor (person, implied) hate him,
how much more do his friends go far from him!
He pursues them with words but does not have them.
— Prov. 19:7

(From King Hezekiah's scribes)
and do not go to your *brother*'s house in the day of your calamity.
Better is a neighbor who is near than a *brother* who is far away.
— Prov. 27:10b

widows אַלְמָנָה (`almanah)

The Hebrew Bible frequently lifts up the widow אַלְמָנָה
(`almanah), the orphan יָתוֹם (yathom) and the sojiurner or
foreigner גֵּר (gar) as those for whom we ought to pay special
concern. This concern is expressed in the Torah or Law in
Deuteronomy, in the Psalms, and in the prophets Jeremiah, Ezekiel
and Zechariah. Interestingly, the Hebrew word used in these
passages for the sojourner or foreigner does not occur in The

Proverbs, in which a similar word זָר *(zar) is used in* "Strangers," *see below.*

but (the Lord) maintains a *widow*'s boundaries.
—   Prov. 15:25b

orphans יָתוֹם (yathom) (modern: orphan)

also: passing away, vanishing חֲלוֹף (halof) (modern: vanishing, ephemeral)
See note above under "Widows."

Do not remove an ancient landmark
or enter the fields of the *fatherless* יְתוֹם;
for their Redeemer is strong;
he will plead their cause against you.
—   Prov. 23:10-11

(From King Lemuel of Massa)
Open your mouth for the dumb
for the cause of all the sons of the *passed away.* חֲלוֹף
—   Prov. 31:8

ancestors
Remove not the ancient landmark which your fathers have set.
—   Prov. 22:28

Do not remove an ancient landmark
—   Prov. 23:10a

Friends, neighbors, strangers, enemies

friends, intimate companions, chief אַלּוּף (`alluf) (modern: general, colonel)

Often defined in biblical genealogies as chief, which explains modern usage.

and a slanderer separates close *friends*.
—   Prov. 16:28b

but he who repeats a matter separates *friends*.
—   Prov. 17:9b

neighbor, companion, friend רֵעַ (re'a) (modern: friend, companion)

Do not say to your *neighbor*,
"Go, and come again, tomorrow I will give it"—-
when you have it with you.
Do not plan evil against your *neighbor*
who dwells trustingly beside you.
—   Prov. 3:28-29

My son, if you have become surety for your *neighbor*,
have given a pledge for a stranger;
if you are snared in the utterance of your lips,
caught in the words of your mouth;
then do this, my son, and save yourself,
for you have come into your *neighbor*'s power;
go, hasten, and importune your *neighbor*.
Give your eyes no sleep and your eyelids no slumber;
save yourself like a gazelle from the hunter,
like a bird from the hand of the fowler.
—   Prov. 6:1-5

So *is* one who has gone in unto the wife of his *neighbor*,
None who do touches her is innocent.
—   Prov. 6:29

With his mouth the ungodly ruins his *neighbor*.
—   Prov. 11:9

He who belittles his *neighbor* lacks sense,
but a man אִישׁ (ish) understanding remains silent.
— Prov. 11:12

The righteous seeks out with his *neighbor,*
but the way of the wicked misleads them.
— Prov. 12:26

The poor is hated even by his *neighbor,*
but lovers of the rich are many.
He who despises his *neighbor* sins,
but he who favors the poor is happy
— Prov. 14:20-21

A man אִישׁ (ish) of violence entices his *neighbor*
and leads him in a way that is not good.
— Prov. 16:29

The *neighbor* loves at all times,
— Prov. 17:17a

A person (אָדָם adam) lacking heart is striking hands (makes a pledge),
a surety he becometh before his *neighbor.*
— Prov. 17:18

The righteous (seems) first in his cause,
but his *neighbor* comes and tests him.
— Prov. 18:17

A man's אִישׁ (ish) *neighbors* may be broken up
but there is one who sticks closer than a brother.
— Prov. 18:24

Wealth adds many *neighbors,*
but the poor is separated from his *neighbors.*
—   Prov. 19:4

and all are friends to a man שׁיאִ (ish) of gifts.
All the brothers of a poor man hate him,
how much more do his friends go far from him!
He pursues them with words but does not have them.
—   Prov. 19:6b-7

The soul of the wicked desires evil,
his *neighbor* finds no grace in his eyes.
—   Prov. 21:10

He who loves purity of heart,
and whose speech is gracious,
will have the king as his *neighbor.*
—   Prov. 22:11

Be not a witness against your *neighbor* without cause,
and do not deceive with your lips.
Do not say, "I will do to him as he has done to me;
I will pay the man שׁיאִ (ish) for what he has done."
—   Prov. 24:28-29

(From King Hezekiah's scribes)
What your eyes have seen do not hastily bring into court;
for what will you do in the end,
when your neighbor puts you to shame?
Argue your case with your *neighbor* himself,
and do not disclose another's secret;
lest he who hears you bring shame upon you,
and your ill repute have no end.
—   Prov. 25:8-10

Let your foot be seldom in your *neighbor*'s house,
lest he become weary of you and hate you.

A man who bears false witness against his *neighbor*
is like a war club, or a sword, or a sharp arrow.
—   Prov. 25:17-18

Like a madman who throws firebrands, arrows, and death,
is the man who deceives his *neighbor*, and says, "Am I not
joking?"
—   Prov. 26:18-19

Ointment and perfume rejoice the heart,
And sweet is one's *friend* — from counsel of the soul.
Your *neighbor*, and your father's *neighbor,* do not forsake
better is a neighbor who is near than a brother who is far away.
—   Prov. 27:9-10

He who blesses his *neighbor* with a loud voice,
rising early in the morning,
will be counted as cursing.
—   Prov. 27:14

A virile man גֶּבֶר (gbr) who flatters his *neighbor*
spreads a net for his feet.
—   Prov. 29:5

<u>companions good and bad</u>

So you will walk in the way of good (persons, implied)
and keep to the paths of the righteous.
—   Prov. 2:20

Do not envy a man אִישׁ (ish) of violence and do not choose any
of his ways
for the perverse man is an abomination to the Lord.
—   Prov. 3:31-32a

One who walks with wise (persons, implied) becomes wise,
but the friend of fools will suffer evil.
— 　Prov. 13:20

Leave the presence of a fool,
for there you do not meet words of knowledge.
— 　Prov. 14:7

Many will beg the nobleman (or philanthropist)
and all are friends of a man אִישׁ (ish) of gifts.
— 　Prov. 19:6

All the brothers of a poor (person, implied) hate him,
how much more do his friends go far from him!
He pursues them with words but does not have them.
— 　Prov. 19:7

A revealer of secrets walks about as a gossip,
do not associate with one who opens his lips.
　— 　Prov. 20:19

Do not associate with a possessor of anger, nor go with a man אִישׁ
(ish)
of wrath, lest you learn his ways and entangle yourself in a snare.
— 　Prov. 22:24-25

See note under "Anger" that the Hebrew word for possessor/lord
is the name of the Canaanite god Baal

Be not among winebibbers, or among gluttonous eaters of meat;
for the drunkard and the glutton will come to poverty,
and drowsiness will clothe one with rags.
— 　Prov. 23:20-21

Be not envious of evil men אִישׁ (ish), nor desire to be with them;
for their minds devise violence and their lips talk of mischief.
— 　Prov. 24:1-2

My son ... do not associate with those (given to) change,
    for suddenly their woe shall rise,

and who knows the ruin that will come from them both?
—   Prov. 24:21-22

(From King Hezekiah's scribes)
Iron sharpens iron,
and a man אִישׁ (ish) sharpens his friends's face.
—   Prov. 27:17

A virile man גֶּבֶר (gbr) who flatters his neighbor
spreads a net for his steps.
—   Prov. 29:5

In transgression an evil man אִישׁ (ish) is snared
—   Prov. 29:6

    <u>nobles, philanthropist</u> נָדִיב (nadiv) (modern: generous,
donor)

*Generous people נדיב, both men and women, brought gold and
silver and fine goods to the Tabrnacle, Num. 35:5 and 22. God
(אֱלֹהִים Elohim) reigns over the nations and nobles of the
peoples gather as the people of the God of Abraham, Psalm 47:9.*

Fine speech is not becoming a fool,
still less is false speech to a *noble*.
—   Prov. 17:7

To impose a fine on the righteous is not good,
and to strike *nobles* for uprightness is not good.
—   Prov. 17:26

A person's אָדָם (adam) gift makes room for him
and brings him before the great.
—   Prov. 18:16

Many will beg the *noble* (or philanthropist)
and all are friends of a man אִישׁ (ish) of gifts.
—   Prov. 19:6

stranger זָאר (zar) (modern: alien, foreign, stranger)

See note under "Widows" above

Lest *strangers* be filled with your power,
And your labours in the house of a foreigner נָכְרִי,
—   Prov. 5:10

My son, if you are surety for your neighbor,
if you struck with a *stranger,*
are you snared with the words of your mouth
are you captured with the words of mouth?
—   Prov. 6:1-2

He who gives surety for a *stranger* will suffer evil,
but he who hates suretyship is secure.
—   Prov. 11:15

The heart knows the bitterness of its soul,
and in its joy a *stranger* does not share.
—   Prov. 14:10

Take a man's garment when he has given surety for a *stranger,*
and hold him in the pledge when he gives surety for foreigners
נָכְרִי
—   Prov. 20:16

(From King Hezekiah's scribes)
Let a *stranger* praise you,
and not your own mouth;
a foreigner נָכְרִי and not your own lips.
—   Prov. 27:2

Take his garment, when a *stranger* hath been surety
And for a foreign נָכְרִי woman pledge it.
—   Prov. 27:13

foreigner, stranger נָכְרִי (nokhri)

Rachel and Leah said they felt treated like foreigners, Gen. 1:15.
Ruth fell on her knees before Boaz and asked why she found favor
in his eyes when she was a foreigner, Ruth 2:10. This word is otfen
used in comparisons with "strange women," see below.)

Lest strangers be filled with your power,
And your labours in the house of a *foreigner* ,
—   Prov. 5:10

Why should you be infatuated, my son,
by a strange woman and hug a *foreigner*'s bosom?
—   Prov. 5:20

For the commandment is a lamp and the law a light,
and the reproofs of discipline are the way of life,
to preserve you from the evil woman,
from the smooth tongue of the *foreigner.*
—   Prov. 6:23-24

For the commandment is a lamp and the law a light,
and the reproofs of discipline are the way of life,
to preserve you from a *strange woman,*
from the *foreign woman's.*
—   Prov. 7:4-5

Take a man's garment when he has given surety for a stranger,
and hold him in the pledge when he gives surety for *foreigners*
—   Prov. 20:16

(From Hezekiah's scribes)
Let a stranger praise you,

and not your own mouth;
a *foreigner* and not your own lips.
— Prov. 27:2

Take his garment, when a stranger hath been surety
and for a *foreign* woman pledge it.
— Prov. 27:13

enemy איב (`oyev) (modern: enemy, foe)

When a man's איש (ish) ways please the Lord (יהוה Yahweh),
He makes even his enemies to be at peace with him.
— Prov. 16:7

Do not rejoice when your enemy falls,
and let not your heart be glad when he stumbles;
lest the Lord (יהוה Yahweh) see it, and be displeased,
and turn away his anger from him.
— Prov. 24:17-18

(From King Hezekiah's scribes)
If your enemy is hungry, give him bread to eat;
and if he is thirsty, give him water to drink;
for you will heap coals of fire on his head,
and the Lord (יהוה Yahweh) will reward you.
— Prov. 25:21-22

Faithful are the wounds of a lover,
profuse are the kisses of a *hated* one.
— Prov. 27:6

adulterer נאף (no`ef)

*Note in the following that any person (אדם adam) is subject to the
temptation of adultery, but it is a virile man (גבר gabor) who is
subject to jealousy. Note also that both genders are capable of
adultery.*

71

Can a man אִישׁ (ish) carry fire in his bosom
and his clothes not be burned?
Or can one walk upon hot coals and his feet not be scorched?
So is he who goes in to his neighbor's wife;
none who touches her will go unpunished.
They do not men despise a thief if he steals
to satisfy his appetite when he is hungry?
And if he is caught, he will pay sevenfold;
he will give all the goods of his house.
He who commits adultery has no sense;
he who does it destroys himself.
Wounds and dishonor will he get,
and his disgrace will not be wiped away.
For jealousy is the burning anger of a virile man גֶּבֶר, (gever)
and he will not spare when he takes revenge.
He will accept no compensation,
nor be appeased though you multiply gifts.
—   Prov. 6:26-35

This is the way of an *adulteress*:
she eats, and wipes her mouth, and says, "I have done no wrong."
—   Prov. 30:20

other women

A dull woman makes noise, simple,
and she knows not what.
—   Prov. 9:13

Every wise woman builds her house
but folly pulls it down with her hands.
—   Prov. 14:1

(From King Lemuel of Massa)
What, my son? What, son of my womb?
What, son of my vows?
Give not your strength to women,

72

your ways to those who destroy kings.
—   Prov. 31:2-3

strange woman, alien זָר (zar)
foreign woman נָכְרִיָּה (nokhrit)

These two terms are often used in the same verse or portion.

You will be saved from the *strange woman*,
from the *foreigner* with her smooth words,
who forsakes the companion of her youth
and forgets the covenant of her God (אֱלֹהִים Elohim)
for her house sinks down to death,
and her paths to the shades;
none who go to her come back
nor do they regain the paths of life.
—   Prov. 2:16-19

For the lips of a *strange woman* drip honey,
and her speech is smoother than oil;
but in the end she is as bitter as wormwood,
sharp as a two-edged sword.
Her feet go down to death,
her steps follow the path to Sheol;
she does not take heed to the path of life;
her ways wander, and she does not know it.
And now, O sons, listen to me,
and do not depart from the words of my mouth.
Keep your way far from her,
and do not go near the door of her house;
lest you give your honor to others and your years to the cruel;
lest *strangers* take their fill of your strength,
and your labors go to a *foreigner*'s house;
and at the end of your life, you groan,
when your flesh and body are consumed,
and you say,

"How I hated discipline, and my heart despised reproof!
I did not listen to the voice of my teachers
or incline my ear to my instructors.
I was at the point of utter ruin in the assembled congregation."
—   Prov. 5:3-14

Why should you be infatuated, my son,
by a *strange woman* and hug a *foreigner*'s bosom?
—   Prov. 5:20

For the commandment is a lamp and the law a light,
and the reproofs of discipline are the way of life,
to preserve you from the evil woman,
from the smooth tongue of the *foreigner*.
—   Prov. 6:23-24

For the commandment is a lamp and the law a light,
and the reproofs of discipline are the way of life,
to preserve you from a *strange woman,*
from the *foreigner*'s smooth words.
—   Prov. 7:4-5

Take his garment, when a stranger hath been surety,
and for a *foreign woman* pledge it.
—   Prov. 27:13

whore זֹנָה (zonah)

For the commandment is a lamp and the law a light,
and the reproofs of discipline ar the way of life,
to preserve you from the evil woman,
from the foreigner's smooth words.
Do not desire her beauty in your heart,
and do not let her capture you with her eyelashes;
for a *whore* may be hired for a loaf of bread,
but another man's אִישׁ (ish) wife hunts for a precious soul.
—   Prov. 6:23-26

For at the window of my house
I have looked out through my lattice,
and I have seen among the simple,
I have perceived among the youths,
a young man without sense,
passing along the street near her corner,
taking the road to her house
in the twilight, in the evening, at the time of night and darkness.
And lo, a woman meets him, dressed as a *whore* wily of heart.
She is loud and wayward, her feet do not stay at home;
now in the street, now in the market,
and at every corner she lies in wait.
She seizes him and kisses him,
and with impudent face she says to him,
"I had to offer sacrifices,
and today I have paid my vows;
so now I have come out to meet you,
to seek you eagerly, and I have found you.
I have decked my couch with coverings,
colored spreads of Egyptian linen;
I have perfumed my bed with myrrh, aloes, and cinnamon.
Come, let us take our fill of love till morning;
let us delight ourselves with love.
For my husband is not at home;
he has gone on a long journey;
he took a bag of money with him;
at full moon he will come home.
With much seductive speech she persuades him;
with her smooth talk she compels him.
All at once he follows her,
as an ox goes to slaughter,
or as a stag is caught fast till an arrow pierces its entrails;
as a bird rushes into a snare;
he does not know it will cost him his life.
And now, O sons, listen to me,
and be attentive to the words of my mouth.
Let not your heart turn aside to her ways,

do not stray into her paths;
for many a victim she has laid low;
yea, all her slain are a mighty host.
Her house is the way to Sheol,
going down to the chambers of death.
—   Prov. 7:4-27

For a *whore* is a deep pit; a foreign woman is a narrow well.
She lies in wait like a robber and increases the faithless among
men.
—   Prov. 23:28

(From King Hezekiah's scribes)
A man אִישׁ   (ish) who loves wisdom makes his father glad,
but a friend of *whores* wastes wealth.
—   Prov. 29:3

      <u>virgin</u> עַלְמָה   (alma) (In modern usage, this is defined as
damsel, girl. The modern word for virgin is בתול (bathol)

*This is the word used in Isaiah 7:14 to predict the birth of Jesus to
a virgin.)*

(From Agur of Massa)
Three things are too wonderful for me;
four I do not understand:
the way of an eagle in the sky, the way of a serpent on a rock,
the way of a ship of the high seas,
and the way of a man with a *virgin.*
—   Prov. 30:18-19

also:
Under three things the earth trembles;
under four it cannot bear up:
when a servant reigns, and when a fool is filled with food;

and a hated one (woman) is married,
and when a maid is heir to her mistress.
—   Prov. 30:21-23

Dynamics of Relating

See also mouth, tongue, lips and words in Chapter 3

gossip and secrets

One despising his neighbor lacks heart,
but a man אִישׁ (ish) of understanding remains silent.
One going with slander is a revealer of secrets,
but the faithful of spirit keeps a matter hidden.
—   Prov. 11:12-13

a slanderer separates close friends.
—   Prov. 16:28

do not disclose another's secret;
lest he who hears you bring shame upon you,
and your ill repute have no end.
—   Prov. 25:9b-10

For lack of wood the fire goes out;
and where there is no whisperer, contention grows silent.
—   Prov. 26:20

the witness

The word false here is שֶׁקֶר *(shkr), meaning lying, deceitful, false. See "deceit" in Chapter 5*

A false witness breathes lies.
—   Prov. 6:19a

but a witness of falsehoods (reveals) deceit.
—   Prov. 12:17

A truthful witness will not lie,
but a false witness lies.
—   Prov. 14:5

A truthful witness delivers souls,
but a deceitful witness, lies.
—   Prov. 14:25

A witness of falsehoods shall not be clean
and a breather of lies shall not escape.
—   Prov. 19:5

A witness of falsehoods shall not be clean,
and a breather of lies shall perish.
—   Prov. 19:9

A worthless witness scorns justice,
—   Prov. 19:28

A false witness will perish,
but a man אִישׁ (ish) that attends will speak forever.
—   Prov. 21:28

Be not a witness against your neighbor without cause,
and do not deceive with your lips.
Do not say, "I will do to him as he has done to me;
I will pay the man אִישׁ (ish) for what he has done."
—   Prov. 24:28-29

Plead your cause with your neighbor,
and the secret of another do not uncover,
lest one who hears your report put you to shame,
and your evil report returns not.
—   Prov. 25:9-10

(Fom King Hezekiah's scribes)
A man אִישׁ (ish) who bears false witness against his neighbor
is like a war club, or a sword, or a sharp arrow.
—   Prov. 25:18

Like a madman who throws firebrands, arrows, and death,
is the man אִישׁ (ish) who deceives his neighbor, and says, "Am I
not joking?"
—   Prov. 26:18-19

betrayer (treachery) בֶּגֶד *(beged)*

The word for treachery is בֶּגֶד *(beged); the modern translation is
the same.*

And in mischief the *treacherous* are captured.
—   Prov. 11:6

and the desire of the *treacherous* is for violence.
—   Prov. 13:2

and the way of the *treacherous is* hard.
—   Prov. 13:15

and the *treacherous* (is a ransom) for the upright.
—   Prov. 21:18b

(From King Hezekiah's scribes)
A bad tooth, and a tottering foot,
is the confidence of the treacherous in a day of adversity.
—   Prov. 25:19

Like a madman who throws firebrands, arrows, and death,
is the man אִישׁ (ish) who deceives his neighbor, and says, "Am I
not joking?"
—   Prov. 26:18-19

A lying tongue hateth its bruised ones,
And a flattering mouth worketh an overthrow!
—   Prov. 26:28

A ruler who is attending to lying words,
 All his ministers ar*e* wicked.
— Prov. 29:12

braggert

(From King Hezekiah's scribes)
Do not boast about tomorrow,
for you do not know what a day may bring forth.
Let another praise you,
and not your own mouth;
a stranger, and not your own lips.
—   Prov. 27:1-2

meddling

Like one who grabs the ears of a dog
is the passerby who enrages himself over strife not his.
—   Prov. 26:17

disputes

quarreling דִּין (din) (The same word is used for plea or
sentence) (no modern usage)

Drive out a scoffer, and contention will go out,
and *quarrels* and ignominy will cease.
—   Prov. 22:10

strife, contention רִיב (riv) (modern: quarrel, fight,
dispute)

Abraham said to Lot, "Let there be no strife between us, " Gen. 13:8

Do not *strive* with a person (אָדָם adam) for no reason,
if he has given you cause.
— Prov. 3:30

but one long to anger calms *strife*,
— Prov. 15:18

Better is a dry piece of bread with quiet
than a house full of sacrifice (i.e., feasting) and *strife*.
— Prov. 17:1

Like the releasing of water is the beginning of *strife*,
so quit the strife before it breaks out.
— Prov. 17:14

A crooked one who loves sin loves *strife*,
— Prov. 17:19a

A fool's lips brings *strife*,
— Prov. 18:6a

It is an honor for a man אִישׁ (ish) to cease from *strife*,
— Prov. 20:3

(From King Hezekiah's scribes)
Like one who grabs the ears of a dog
is the passerby who enrages himself over *strife* not his.
— Prov. 26:17

As charcoal to hot embers and wood to fire,
so a contentious man for kindling *strife*.
— Prov. 26:21

strife דִּין (also defined as debate, judgment, cause, please)

Not found in modern usage. The only other uses in the Hebrew
Bible, in Numbers and Leviticus, are for ceremonial purposes.

A vain one through pride causes *strife*.
— Prov. 13:10

Whoso is loving sin is loving *strife*
— Prov. 17:19

 also:

(From King Hzekiah's scribes)
If a wise man (אִישׁ ish) disputes with a foolish man (אִישׁ ish),
he even shakes or laughs and there is no rest.
— Prov. 29:9

Chapter 3: OUR TONGUES AND BODIES

Longevity

Note that the phrase "fountain of life" occurs several times in Proverbs as well as Psalm 36:9

My son, do not forget my law,
but let your heart keep my commandments;
for length of days and years of life and peace will they give you.
—   Prov. 3:1-2

Long life is in her right hand; in her left hand are riches and honor.
Her ways are ways of pleasantness,
and all her paths are peace.
She is a tree of life to those who lay hold of her;
those who hold her fast are called happy.
—   Prov. 3:16-18

Hear, my son, and accept my words.
that the years of your life may be many.
—   Prov. 4:10

For he who finds me finds life and obtains favor from the Lord
(יהוה Yahweh);
but he who misses me injures himself;
all who hate me love death.
—   Prov. 8:35-36

For by me your days will be multiplied,
and years will be added to your life.
—   Prov. 9:11

The mouth of the righteous is a fountain of life,
—Prov. 10:11

In the path of righteousness is life,
and the way of that path is not death.
—   Prov. 12:28

He who guards his mouth preserves his life,
—   Prov. 13:3a

but the tree of life is fulfilled passion.
—   Prov. 13:12b

The law of the wise is a fountain of life
that one may avoid the snares of death.
—   Prov. 13:14

There is a way (seeming) upright to a man (אָדָם ish)
but its end is the ways of death.
—   Prov. 14:12

The fear of the Lord (יהוה Yahweh) is a fountain of life,
that one may avoid the snares of death.
—   Prov. 14:27

but the righteous finds refuge in his death.
—   Prov. 14:32b

but he who hates bribes will live.
—   Prov. 15:27b

A fountain of life is understanding to its possessors,
—   Prov. 16:22

Death and life are in the hand (power) of the tongue,
and those who love it will eat its fruits.
—   Prov. 18:21

He who keeps the commandment keeps his life,
and he who despises His ways will die.
—   Prov. 19:16

The fear of the Lord (יהוה Yahweh) leads to life,
—   Prov. 19:23a

and he who has it rests satisfied,
he will not be visited with evil.
—   Prov. 19:23

Strength

> strength, mighty, fierce עז ('oz) (modern: strong, fierce,
> sharp, intense)

*Strength is used here in a variety of ways – physical strength,
strength of counsel, strength of the Lord. For instance, "The Lord
(יְהוָה Yahweh) is the strength of my life," Psalm 27:1*

Strength to the upright is the way of the Lord (יהוה Yahweh),
—   Prov. 10:29a

A wise scales the city of the mighty (גִּבּוֹר gevorah)
and topples the *strength* it trusts in.
—   Prov. 21:22

A wise man (גִּבּוֹר gbr) (or warrior) is strengthened,
a man (יהוה ish) of knowledge firms up strength;
—   Prov. 24:5

(From Agur of Massa)
The ants are a people not *strong,*

yet they provide their food in the summer;
— Prov. 30:25

(From King Lemuel of Massa)
She (a good wife) has girded her loins with *strength,*
— Prov. 31:17a

Strength and dignity are her clothing,
— Prov. 31:25

    <u>strength, vigor, power</u> כֹּחַ (koakh) (modern: force, power, strength)

This is the strength that Samson used to bring down the house of the Philistines, Judges 16

Where there are no cattle the manger is clean,
by there is much increase by the *stength* of the ox.
— Prov. 14:4

In the fear of the Lord (יהוה Yahweh) is *strong* confidence,
— Pov. 14:26

A tower of *strength* is the name of the Lord (יהוה Yahweh)
— Prov. 18:10

A brother offended is like a city of *strength,*
— Prov. 18:19

The glory of young men is their *vigor,*
— Prov. 20:29

A city of the mighty hath the wise gone up,
And bringeth down the *strength* of its confidence.
— Prov. 21:22

A mighty man is wise in strength,
And a man of knowledge firms up might.
— Prov. 24:5

If you faint in the day of adversity, narrow is your *strength.*
— Prov. 24:10

strength, valor, might גְּבוּרָה (gevorah) (modern: stength)

*Note the relationship to the word גִּבּוֹר. "Thou hast a mighty arm;
strong is thy hand, high thy right hand," Psalm 89:13. In this
verse, and in Prov. 21:22 below, mighty is the translation of
גְּבוּרָה and strong is a translation of עֹז*

Mine *is* counsel and practical wisdom,
understanding to me is *might.*
— Prov. 8:14

A city of the *mighty* hath the wise gone up,
And bringeth down the strength of its confidence.
— Prov. 21:22

strength, power, valor, army חַיִל (chil)(modern: strength,
power, army)

*This word is used frequently in the historical books of the Hebrew
Bible with heroic connotations, as in Jephthah the judge was "a
mighty man of valor," Judges 11:1*

A woman of *valor* is a crown to her husband,
— Prov. 12:4

Give not to women thy *valor,*
And thy ways to wiping away of kings.
— Prov. 31:3

Our Body

When a verse mentions more than one part of a body, it is placed in this section.

Be not wise in your own eyes;
fear the Lord and turn away from evil.
It will be healing to your navel and moisture to your bones.
—   Prov. 3:6-8

For the lips of a strange woman drip honey,
and her speech is smoother than oil;
but in the end she is as bitter as wormwood,
sharp as a two-edged sword.
Her feet go down to death,
her steps follow the path to Sheol;
she does not take heed to the path of life;
her ways wander, and she does not know it.
—   Prov. 5:3-6

A little sleep, a little slumber,
a little folding of the hands to rest,
and your poverty will come as one stalking,
and your want as a shield of man (אִישׁ ish).
—   Prov. 6:10-11

A worthless person (אָדָם adam), an evil man (אִישׁ ish),
walks with a crooked mouth, winking with his eyes,
scraping with his feet, pointing with his fingers,
froward things are in his heart...
—   Prov. 6:12-14a

There are six things which the Lord hates,
seven which are an abomination to him:
haughty eyes, a false tongue,
and hands that shed innocent blood,
a heart that devises wicked plans,

feet that make haste to run to evil,
a false witness who breathes out lies,
and one who sows discord among brothers.
—   Prov. 6:16-19

My son, keep your father's commandment,
and forsake not your mother's law...
When you walk, they will lead you;
when you lie down, they will watch over you;
and when you awake, they will talk with you.
For the commandment is a lamp and the law a light,
and the reproofs of discipline are the way of life,
to preserve you from the strange woman,
from the foreigner's smooth words.
Do not desire her beauty in your heart,
and do not let her capture you with her eyelashes;
for a whore may be hired for a loaf of bread,
but another man's ((אִישׁ ish) wife hunts for a precious soul.
—   Prov. 6:20-26

My son, keep my words and treasure up my commandments with
you;
keep my commandments and live,
keep my law as the apple of your eye;
bind them on your fingers,
write them on the tablet of your heart.
—   Prov. 7:1-3

In the sin of the lips is the snare of evil,
but from distress will emerge the righteous.
From the fruit of a man's (אִישׁ ish) mouth is he satisfied with
good,
and the dealing of a man's (אִישׁ ish) hands will return to him.
The way of a fool is right in his own eyes,
—   Prov. 12:13-15a

To life a heart of flesh is healing,
but the rottenness of bones is envy.
— Prov. 14:30

The light of the eyes rejoices the heart,
and good news makes the bone fat.
— Prov. 15:30

The lamp of the Lord is the breath of a person (אָדָם adam),
searching all the innermost parts of the belly.
— Prov. 20:27

(From King Hezekiah's scribes)
Like a bad tooth and a slipping foot
is trust in a traitor in a day of distress.
— Prov. 25:19

(From Agur of Massa)
O generation, how lofty are its eyes,
and its eyelids are lifted up.
A generation whose swords are its teeth, and knives its jaw,
to devour the afflicted from the earth
and the destitute from among men (אָדָם adam).
— Prov. 30:12-13

Bones

There are two words for bone in the Proverbs.

עֶצֶם ('etsem)
but rottenness is his *bones* is like (a woman) causing shame.
— Prov. 12:4

but the rottenness of *bones* is envy.
— Prov. 14:30

and good news makes the *bone* fat.
— Prov. 15:30

גֶּרֶם (gerem)

a downcast spirit dries up the *bone*.
— Prov. 17:22b

(From King Hezekiah's scribes)
And a soft tongue breaketh a *bone*.
— Prov. 25:15

Head   רֹאשׁ (r`osh) (modern: head, leader, chief, start, as in Rosh Hashana, the start of the JewIsh New Year, or the chief of bureau)

Hear, my son, your father's instruction,
and reject not your mother's teaching;
for they are a fair garland for your *head*,
and pendants for your neck.
— Prov. 1:8-9

Get wisdom, and whatever you get, get understanding.
Prize her highly, and she will exalt you;
she will honor you if you embrace her;
she will bestow on you a beautiful crown.
— Prov. 4:7-9

Blessed are the *head* of the righteous,
but the wicked's mouth covers violence.
— Prov. 10:6

The plans of the heart are for a person (אָדָם adam),
but the answer of the tongue is from the Lord (יהוה Yahweh).
— Prov. 16:1

As the waters of streams,
a king's heart is in the hands of the Lord (יהוה Yahweh).⁵
wherever He desires he inclines it.
Every way of a man אִישׁ (ish) is right in his eyes,
but the Lord (יהוה Yahweh) weighs the heart.
—   Prov. 21:1-2

Lifted eyes and a proud heart,
the lamp of the wicked, are sin.
—   Prov. 21:4

My son, give me your heart,
and let your eyes watch my ways.
—   Prov. 23:26

(From King Hezekiah's scribes)
If your enemy is hungry, give him bread to eat,
and if he is thirsty, give him water to drink,
for coals (of fire) you will heap on his head.
—   Prov. 25:22

Gray hair   שֵׂיבָה (sevah) (modern: old age, gray hair)

"At the presence of gray hairs thou dost rise up, and thou hast honoured the presence of an old man, and hast been afraid of thy God; I am the Lord (יהוה Yahweh),". – Leviticus 19:32 "Even to old age I am He, and to gray hairs I carry, I made, and I bear, yea, I carry and deliver," Isaiah 46:4

Gray hair is a crown of glory,
it is gained in a righteous life.
—   Prov. 16:31

The glory of young men is their vigor,
and the beauty of old men is their *gray hair*.
—   Prov. 20:27

Face פָּנִים (panim) (modern: face)

And she (a whore) seizes him and kisses him;
she hardens her face.
—   Prov. 7:13

As vinegar to the teeth, and smoke to the eyes,
so the lazy one to them that send him.
—   Prov. 10:26

A joyful heart makes a good *face,*
but by the pain of heart the spirit is broken.
—   Prov. 15:13

The hearing ear and the seeing eye,
the Lord (יהוה Yahweh)has made them both.
Love not sleep, lest you become a poor one,
open your eyes and you will have plenty of bread.
—   Prov. 20:12-13

A wicked man (ish) hardens his face,
—   Prov. 21:29a

In the ears of a dullard do not speak,
for he will despise the good sense of your words.
—   Prov. 23:9

To discern *faces* in judgment is not good (i.e., to show partiality)
—   Prov. 24:23 (see Prov. 28:21 below)

(From King Hezekiah's scribes)
As in water face answers to *face,*
so the mind of person (אָדָם adam) to person (אָדָם adam)
 Sheol and Abaddon are never satisfied,
and never satisfied are the eyes of a person (אָדָם adam).
—   Prov. 27:19-20

To discern *faces* is not good
—   Prov. 28:21 (see Prov. 24:23 above)

(From Agur of Massa)
There are those who curse their fathers
and do not bless their mothers.
There are those who are pure in their own eyes
but are not cleansed of their filth.
There are those – how lofty are their eyes,
how high their eyelids lift!
There are those whose teeth are swords, whose teeth are knives,
to devour the poor from off the earth,
the needy from among people (אָדָם adam).
—   Prov. 30:11-14

Eye עַיִן ('ayin)

Let your *eyes* look directly forward,
and your gaze be straight before you.
—   Prov. 4:25

Give not sleep to your *eyes*,
or slumber to your eyelids.
—   Prov. 6:4

The *eyes* of the Lord (יהוה Yahweh) are in every place,
keeping watch on the evil and the good.
—   Prov. 15:3

He who winks his *eyes* plans perverse things,
—   Prov. 16:30a

but the *eyes* of a fool are on the ends of the earth.
—   Prov. 17:24

A king who sits on the throne of judgment
winnows all evil with his *eyes*.
—   Prov. 20:8

Every way of a man (אִישׁ ish) is right in his *eyes*,
but the Lord (יהוה Yahweh)weighs the heart.
—   Prov. 21:2

Lifted *eyes* and a proud heart,
the lamp of the wicked, are sin.
—   Prov. 21:4

The soul of the wicked desireth evil,
his neighbor findeth no favor in his *eyes*.
—   Prov. 21:10

The *eyes* of the Lord (יהוה Yahweh) preserve knowledge,
—   Prov. 22:12

Will your *eyes* fly (fix) on it, and it is not?
For it will surely make wings for itself like an eagle
and fly into the heavens.
—   Prov. 23:5

My son, give me your heart,
and let your eyes watch my ways.
—   Prov. 23:26

(From King Hezekiah's scribes)
What your *eyes* have seen do not hastily bring into court;
for what will you do in the end,
when your neighbor puts you to shame?
—   Prov. 25:7a-8

He who gives to the poor has no lack,
but he that hides his *eyes*, many curses.
—   Prov. 28:27

The poor and a man of injuries meet together,
but the Lord (יהוה Yahweh) enlightens the *eyes* of both.
— Prov. 29:13

Ear אֹזֶן (`ozen) (modern: the Hebrew word for "balance" is very similar, reminding that the ear is essential for balance)

So bow your *ear* to wisdom,
you shall extend your heart to understanding.
— Prov. 2:2

My son, listen ... and bow your *ear*,
— Prov. 4:20, 5:1

The *ear* that hears the correction of life will abide in wisdom.
— Prov. 15:31

The heart of the intelligent gets knowledge,
and the *ear* of the wise seeks knowledge.
— Prov. 18:15

One who shuts his *ear* at the cry of the weak,
shall he himself also call and not be heard?
— Prov. 21:13

Stretch your *ears* and hear the words of the wise,
and apply your heart to my knowledge.
— Prov. 22:17

Bring in for discipline your heart
and your *ears* to the words of knowledge.
— Prov. 23:12

(From King Hezekiah's scribes)
As a gold ring and a gold item,
so a wise reprover on a hearing *ear*.
— Prov. 25:12

One who turns aside his *ear* from hearing the law,
even his prayer is an abomination.
—   Prov. 28:9

Mouth, tongue, lips (i.e., our words)
*(These are references to our words. See also "The Witness" in
Chapter 2.)*

Put away from you crooked speech,
and put devious talk far from you.
—   Prov. 4:24

My son! if you have been surety for thy friend,
have stricken for a stranger your hand,
if you are snared in the utterance of your lips,
caught in the words of your mouth;
then do this, my son, and save yourself,
for you have come into your neighbor's power:
go, hasten, and importune your neighbor.
—   Prov. 6:1-3

She lured him with her word,
with flattery she forced him.
—   Prov. 7:21

Hear, for I will speak noble things,
and from my lips will come what is right;
for my mouth will utter truth;
wickedness is an abomination to my lips.
All the words of my mouth are righteous;
there is nothing twisted or crooked in them.
They are all straight to him who understands
and right to those who find knowledge.
—   Prov. 8:6-9

and a froward mouth I hate.
—   Prov. 8:13b

Blessings are to the head of the righteous,
but the wicked's mouth conceals violence.
— Prov. 10:6

The mouth of the righteous is a fountain of life,
but the wicked's mouth conceals violence.
— Prov. 10:11

On the lips of him who has understanding, wisdom is found,
but a rod is for the back of him who lacks sense.
The wise store up knowledge but the fool's mouth – ruin is near.
— Prov. 10:13-14

He who conceals hatred has lying lips,
and he who utters slander is a fool.
When words are many, transgression is not lacking,
but he who restrains his lips is prudent.
The tongue of the righteous is choice silver;
the mind of the wicked is of little worth.
The lips of the righteous feed many.
— Prov. 10:18-21a

The mouth of the righteous brings forth wisdom,
but the tongue of the froward (or perverse) will be cut off.
The lips of the righteous know what is pleasing,
but the mouth of the wicked, what is perverse.
— Prov. 10:31-32

With his mouth a godless one would destroy his neighbor.
— Prov. 11:9a

He who belittles his neighbor lacks sense,
but a man (אִישׁ ish) of understanding remains silent.
He goes about as a talebearer reveals secrets,
but he who is trustworthy in spirit keeps a thing hidden.
— Prov. 11:12-13

By the mouth of his good sense a man (אִישׁ ish) shall be praised,
—   Prov. 12:8a

In the sin of the lips is the snare of evil,
—   Prov. 12:13a

From the fruit of a man's (אִישׁ ish) mouth he is satisfied with good,
—   Prov. 12:14

He who speaks the truth gives honest evidence,
but a false witness utters deceit.
There is one whose rash words are like sword thrusts,
but the tongue of the wise brings healing.
Truthful lips endure forever,
but a lying tongue is for a moment.
—   Prov. 12:17-19

Lying lips are an abomination to the Lord (יהוה Yahweh),
but those who do truth are his delight.
—   Prov. 12:22

but a good word makes him glad.
—   Prov. 12:25b

From the fruit of a man's (אִישׁ ish) mouth he eats good,
—   Prov. 13:2a (see Prov. 18:20-21 below)

He who guards his mouth preserves his life,
he who opens wide his lips comes to ruin.
—   Prov. 13:3

The talk of a stupid one is a rod of pride,
but the lips of the wise will preserve them.
—   Prov. 14:3

Go from a dull man (אִישׁ ish)
or you will not know the lips of knowledge.
— Prov. 14:7

In all toil there is profit,
but the word of lips (tends) to poverty.
— Prov. 14:23

A soft answer turns away burning anger,
but a harsh word stirs up anger.
The tongue of the wise makes knowledge good,
but the mouth of fools.
— Prov. 15:1-2

A healing tongue is a tree of life,
but perversity in its breaks the spirit.
— Prov. 15:4

The lips of the wise spread knowledge,
but not the heart of fools.
— Prov. 15:7

but the mouths of fools feed on folly.
— Prov. 15:14b

A man (אִישׁ ish) has joy by the answer of his mouth,
and a word in its time, how good it is.
— Prov. 15:23

the words of the pure are pleasing to him (the Lord).
— Prov. 15:26b

The heart of the righteous ponders how to answer,
but the mouth of the wicked pours out evil things.
— Prov. 15:28

The plans of the heart are for a person (אָדָם adam),
but the answer of the tongue is from the Lord (יהוה Yahweh).
— Prov. 16:1

Inspired decisions are on the lips of the king,
in justice his mouth is not a traitor.
— Prov. 16:10

Righteous lips are the delight of kings,
and he loves him who speaks uprightly.
— Prov. 16:13

and sweetness of lips increases persuasion.
— Prov. 16:21b

The heart of the wise makes his mouth insightful,
and adds persuasiveness to his lips.
Pleasant words are like a honeycomb,
sweetness to the soul and healing to the body.
— Prov. 16:23-24

A worthless man's (אִישׁ ish) speech is like a scorching fire.
— Prov. 16:27b

and a whisperer separates close friends.
— Prov. 16:28b

An evil-doer listens to evil lips,
and a liar gives heed to a tongue of evil desire.
— Prov. 17:4

Fine speech is not becoming a fool,
still less is false speech to a prince.
— Prov. 17:7

and one perverse in his tongue falls into evil.
— Prov. 17:20b

He who restrains his words has knowledge,
—   Prov. 17:27a

Even a fool who keeps silent is considered wise,
when he closes his lips, he is thought (to be) understanding.
—   Prov. 17:28

A fool takes no pleasure in understanding,
but only in expressing his opinion.
—   Prov. 18:2

the words of a man's (אִישׁ ish) mouth are deep waters,
the fountan of wisdom is a gushing stream.
—   Prov. 18:4

A dullard's lips enter into strife,
and his mouth invites a flogging.
A dullard's mouth is his ruin,
and his lips are a snare to himself.

The words of a backbiter are like delicious morsels,
they go down into the inner parts of the body.
—   Prov. 18:6-8

If one gives an answer before he hears,
it is his folly and shame.
—   Prov. 18:13

The first (to state his case) seems right,
until his neighbor comes and tests him.
—   Prov. 18:17

From the fruit of his mouth a man (אִישׁ ish) is satisfied,
he is satisfied by the yield of his lips.
Death and life are in the hand (power) of the tongue,
and those who love it will eat its fruits.
—   Prov. 18:20-21 (see Prov. 13:2a above)

Better is a poor one who walks in his integrity
than one who is crooked in speech and a fool.
—   Prov. 19:1

A false witness will not go unpunished,
and he who utters a lie will not escape.
—   Prov. 19:9

A worthless witness scoffs at justice,
and the mouth of the wicked devours evil.
—   Prov. 19:28

but the lips of knowledge are a precious jewel.
—   Prov. 20:15

Bread gained by a lie is sweet to a man (אִישׁ ish),
but afterward his mouth will be full of gravel.
—   Prov. 20:17

A revealer of secrets walks about as a gossip,
do not associate with one who opens his lips.
—   Prov. 20:19

It is a snare for a person (אָדָם adam) to say rashly, "It is holy,"
and after to inquire about his vows.
—   Prov. 20:25

The getting of treasures by a lying tongue
is hot air (vanity) driven by those seeking death.
—   Prov. 21:6

He who keeps his mouth and his tongue
keeps his soul from distresses.
—   Prov. 21:23

A false witness will perish,
but a man (אִישׁ ish) that attends will speak forever.
— Prov. 21:28

One who loves purity of heart,
and whose speech is gracious,
will have the king as his friend.
The eyes of the Lord (יהוה Yahweh) keep watch over knowledge,
but he overthrows the words of the faithless.
— Prov. 22:11-12

The mouth of a loose woman is a deep pit;
those hated by the Lord (יהוה Yahweh) will fall into it.
— Prov. 22:14

For it will be pleasant if you keep them (the words of wisdom)
within you,
if all of them are on your lips.
— Prov. 22:18

Do not speak in the hearing of a fool,
for he will despise the wisdom of your words.
— Prov. 23:9

My soul will rejoice when your lips speak what is right.
— Prov. 23:16

For violence their hearts meditate,
and mischief, their lips.
— Prov. 24:2

Wisdom is too high for a stupid one,
in the gate does he not open his mouth?
— Prov. 24:7

One kisses the lips that return straight words.
— Prov. 24:26

Be not a witness against your neighbor without cause,
and do not deceive with your lips.
Do not say, "I will do to him as he has done to me;
I will pay the man (אִישׁ ish) for what he has done."
—   Prov. 24:28-29

(From King Hezekiah's scribes)
do not disclose another's secret;
lest he who hears you bring shame upon you,
and your ill repute have no end.
—   Prov. 25:9b-10

A word fitly spoken is like apples of gold in a setting of silver,
Like a gold ring or an ornament of gold
is a wise reprover to a listening ear.
Like the cold of snow in the time of harvest
is a faithful messenger to those who send him,
he refreshes the spirit of his masters.
Like clouds and wind without rain
is a man who boasts of a gift he does not give.
With patience a ruler may be persuaded,
and a soft tongue will break a bone.
—   Prov. 25:11-15

A man (אִישׁ ish) who bears false witness against his neighbor
is like a war club, or a sword, or a sharp arrow.
—   Prov. 25:18

The north wind brings forth rain;
and a backbiting tongue, angry looks.
—   Prov. 25:23

Weak are the legs of the lame,
so is a proverb in the mouth of dullards.
—   Prov. 26:7

A thorn goes into a drunk's hand,
and a proverb in the mouth of dullards.
— Prov. 26:9

For lack of wood the fire goes out;
and where there is no whisperer, quarreling ceases.
As charcoal to hot embers and wood to fire,
so is a contentious man (אִישׁ ish) for kindling strife.
The words of a whisperer are like delicious morsels;
they go down into the inner parts of the body.
Like the glaze covering an earthen vessel
are smooth lips with an evil heart.
He who hates, dissembles with his lips
and harbors deceit in his heart;
though his hatred be covered with guile,
his wickedness will be exposed in the assembly.
He who digs a pit will fall into it,
and a stone will come back upon him who starts it rolling.
A lying tongue hates its victims,
and a flattering mouth works ruin.
— Prov. 26:20-28

Let another praise you,
and not your own mouth;
a stranger, and not your own lips.
— Prov. 27:2

He who rebukes a person (אָדָם adam) will afterward find more favor
than he who flatters with his tongue.
— Prov. 28:23

Do you see a man ((אִישׁ ish) hasty in his words?
There is more hope for a fool than for him.
— Prov. 29:20

(From Agur of Massa)
Do not slander a servant to his master,
lest he curse you and you be held guilty.
—   Prov. 30:10

If you have been foolish, exalting yourself,
or if you have plotting, put your hand on your mouth.
—   Prov. 30:32

(From King Lemuel of Massa)
Open your mouth for the dumb,
for the rights of all the orphans.
Open your mouth, judge righteously,
and defend the afflicted and the destitute.
—   Prov. 31:8-9

She (a good wife) opens her mouth in wisdom
and the law of mercy is on her tongue.
—   Prov. 31:26

Neck גַּרְגְּרֹת (gargereth)

Hear, my son, your father's instruction,
and reject not your mother's teaching;
for they are a fair garland for your head,
and pendants for your *neck.*
—   Prov. 1:8-9

Let not truth and mercy forsake you;
bind them about your *neck,*
write them on the tablet of your heart.
So you will find favor and good repute in the sight of God and
person.
—   Prov. 3:3-4

My son, keep sound wisdom and discretion;
let them not escape from your sight,

and they will be life for your soul and adornment for your *neck*.
—   Prov. 3:21-22

My son, keep your father's commandment,
and forsake not your mother's law.
Bind them upon your heart always;
tie them about your *neck*.
—   Prov. 6:20-21

(From King Hezekiah's scribes)
A man (אִישׁ ish) of correction who suddenly stiffens his neck
will be shattered and will not be healed.
—   Prov. 29:2

Hand יָד (yad)

*How mighty the hand and great the fear which Moses wielded
before the eyes of all Israel, Deueronomy 34:12*

and the word of a person's (אָדָם adam) *hands* will return to him.
—   Prov. 12:14

Wise women build a house
but folly tears it down with her *hands*.
—   Prov. 14:1

The desire of the lazy one kills him
for his *hands* refuse to labor.
—   Prov. 21:25

(From King Lemuel of Massa)
and (a good wife) works her palms in delight.
—   Prov. 31:13b

from the fruit of her palms she plants a vineyard.
—   Prov. 31:16b

She puts her *hands* on the distaff
and her palms hold the spindle.
She extends her palms to the afflicted
And her hands she reaches out to the destitute.
—   Prov. 31:19-20

Give to her of the fruit of her *hands*.
—   Prov. 31:31a

Heart לֵב (lev) (modern: heart)

The following list is not complete. See earlier reference.

Trust in the Lord with all your *heart*,
and do not rely on your understanding.
—   Prov. 3:5

Keep your *heart* with all viligance;
for from it flows the springs of life.
—   Prov. 4:23

My son, keep your father's commandment,
and forsake not your mother's teaching.
Bind them upon your *heart* always;
tie them about your neck.
—   Prov. 6:20-21

Hope deferred makes the *heart* sick,
—   Prov. 13:12a

The *heart* knows its soul of bitterness,
and with its joy a stranger does not meddle.
—   Prov. 14:10

Even in laughter the *heart* is pained,
and the end of joy is grief.
—   Prov. 14:13

Hell and destruction are open before the Lord (יהוה Yahweh),
how much more the *hearts* of the sons of persons (אָדָם adam)?
—   Prov. 15:11

A joyful heart makes a good face,
but by the pain of *heart* the spirit is broken.
—   Prov. 15:13a

but goodness of *heart* is a continual feast.
—   Prov. 15:15b

Folly is joy to him who lacks *heart*,
—   Prov. 15:21a

The *heart* of the righteous ponders how to answer,
—   Prov. 15:28a

but he who heeds correction gets *heart*.
—   Prov. 15:32b

A person's (אָדָם adam) *heart* plans his way,
but the Lord (יהוה Yahweh) directs his steps.
—   Prov. 16:9

and the Lord (יהוה Yahweh) tries *hearts.*
—   Prov. 17:3b

A joyful *heart* makes good healing,
—   Prov. 17:22a

Before destruction a man's (אִישׁ ish) *heart* is haughty,
but humility goes before honor.
—   Prov. 18:12

The *heart* of the prudent gets knowledge,
and the ear of the wise seeks knowledge.
—   Prov. 18:15

The folly of a person (אָדָם adam) brings his way to ruin,
and his *heart* rages against the Lord (יהוה Yahweh).
—   Prov. 19:3

He who gets *heart* loves his own soul,
—   Prov. 19:8a

Many are the purposes in a man's (אִישׁ ish) heart,
but the counsel of the Lord (יהוה Yahweh) will rise (prevail).
—   Prov. 19:21

Like deep water is counsel in a man's (אִישׁ ish) *heart,*
—   Prov. 20:5a

Who can say, "I have made my *heart* pure,
I am cleansed from my sin"?
—   Prov. 20:9

Blows that wound cleanse away evil,
and strokes, the chambers of the *heart.*
—   Prov. 20:30

My son, if your *heart* is wise, my *heart* too will be glad.
—   Prov. 23:15

Let not your *heart* envy sinners,
but continue in the fear of the Lord (יהוה Yahweh) all the day.
—   Prov. 23:17

If you say, "Behold, we did not know this,"
does not he who weighs the hearts perceive it?
Does not the Keeper of your soul know,
and will he not repay each person (אָדָם adam) according to his
work"?
—   Prov. 24:12

<u>Foot</u> רֶגֶל (regel) (modern: foot, leg)

My son, do not walk in the way of them,
hold back your *foot* from their paths;
for their feet run to evil,
and they make haste to shed blood.
—   Prov. 1:15-16

In all your ways acknowledge him,
and he will make straight your paths.
—   Prov. 3:6

Then you will walk on your way securely
and your *foot* will not stumble.
If you sit down, you will not be afraid;
when you lie down your sleep will be sweet.
Do not be afraid of sudden panic
or of the ruin of the wicked, when it comes;
for the Lord will be your confidence
and will keep your *foot* from being caught.
—   Prov. 3:23-26

I have taught you the way of wisdom;
I have led you in the paths of uprightness.
When you walk, your step will not be hampered,
and if you run, you will not stumble.
—   Prov. 4:11

Do not enter the path of the wicked,
and do not walk in the way of evil men.
Avoid it; do not go on it and pass on.
For they cannot sleep unless they have done wrong;
they are robbed of sleep unless they have made some one stumble.
For they eat the bread of wickedness and drink the win of violence.
But the path of the righteous is like the light of dawn,
which shines brighter and brighter until full day.
The way of the wicked is like deep darkness;

they do not know over what they stumble.
—   Prov. 4:14-19

Take heed to the path of your feet,
then all your ways will be sure.
Do not swerve to the right or to the left;
turn your foot away from evil.
—   Prov. 4:26-27

Her feet go down to death,
her steps follow the path to Sheol.
—   Prov. 5:5, referring to a strange woman.

For before the eyes of the Lord (יהוה Yahweh) are a man's (אִישׁ
ish) ways,
and he watches all his paths.
—   Prov. 5:21

Or can one walk on hot coals
and his feet not be burned?
So is he who goes in to his neighbor's wife.
—   Prov. 6:28-29a

Her (a whore's) feet do not stay at home.
—   Prov. 7:11

A person's (אָדָם adam) heart plans his way,
but the Lord (יהוה Yahweh) directs his step.
—   Prov. 16:9

and he rushing with his feet, sins.
—   Prov. 19:2

The steps of the pure-hearted are ordered by the Lord (יהוה
Yahweh)
how then can a prson (אָדָם adam) discern his way?
—   Prov. 20:24

(From King Hezekiah's scribes)
He cuts off (his) feet and drinks violence
who sends messages by the hand of a dullard.
—   Prov. 26:6

A man (אִישׁ ish) who flatters his neighbor
spreads a net for his steps.
—   Prov. 29:5

Chapter 4: GODLY TRAITS

<u>BLESSED</u>

 <u>blessed, benediction</u> בָּרךְ (barukh) (modern: blessing, greeting))

but on the abode of the righteous,
He (the Lord) (יהוה Yahweh) *blesses.*
—   Prov. 3:33

Let your fountain be *blessed,*
—   Prov. 5:18a

Blessings are on the head of the righteous,
...
The memory of the righteous is a *blessing,*
—   Prov. 10:6a, 7a

The *blessing* of the Lord (יהוה Yahweh) makes it upright,
—   Prov. 10:22

By the *blessing* of the upright is lifted up a city,
—   Prov. 11:11

The one who scatters (gives freely) increases the more,
but the withholder of rightness comes only to poverty.
The *blessing* of the soul shall be made fat,
and he watering will also drink fully.
—   Prov. 11:24

People will curse the old holding back grain,
but a *blessing* to the head of the one selling grain.
—   Prov. 11:26

An inheritance gotten hastily in the beginning
but the end of it shall not be *blessed.*
—   Prov. 20:21

The eye of the good – he will be *blessed,*
for he gives bread to the poor.
—   Prov. 22:9

But to those who rebuke (the wicked one) it is pleasant,
and on them comes a *blessing.*
—   Prov. 24:25

(From King Hezekiah's scribes)
One who *blesses* his friend with a loud voice in the morning,
rising early, it will be deemed cursing.
—   Prov. 27:14

A faithful man (ish) shall be full of blessings
—   Prov. 28:20

(From Agur of Massa)
A generation that curses its father and does not *bless* its mother.
—   Prov. 30:11

blessed, happy אַשְׁרֵי (`ashre)

See as Happy, blessed in Chapter I: Our Emotions

Cover, conceal כָּסָה (kasah) (modern: cover)

*Notice that a word drawn from ordinary usage is used in both a
positive and negative way – to "cover" sin in what some English
versions translate as "forgiveness" and to "cover" hatred" in a*

beguiling way. It is the same word used when Noah's sons covered him in his drunkeness, Gen. 9:23.

the mouth of the wicked *covers* violence.
—   Prov. 10:6b, 11b

Hatred stirs up contention,
but loves *covers* all offenses.
—   Prov. 10:12

He who *covers* hatred (has) falsehood of lips,
and one sending out slander is a fool.
—   Prov. 10:18

One going with slander is a revealer of secrets,
but the faithful of spirit *covers* a matter.
—   Prov. 11:13

but the astute *cover* shame.
—   Prov. 12:16b

an astute person (אָדָם adam) *covers* knowledge.
—   Prov. 12:23

A king's burning anger is a messenger of death,
and a wise man (אִישׁ ish) *covers* it.
—   Prov. 16:14

He who *covers* (i.e., forgives) a sin seeks love,
but he who repeats a matter separates friends.
—   Prov. 17:9

And lo, all of it (a lazy man's (אִישׁ ish) vineyard) was grown up
with thistles, nettles *covered* its surface, and it stone wall was
broken down.
—   Prov. 24:31

The glory of God is to *cover* a matter,
— Prov. 25:2

(From King Hezekiah's scribes)
Hatred is *covered* by guile,
his evil shall be revealed in the assembly.
— Prov. 26:26

Discerning, judicious, astute מֵבִין (mevin) (modern:
understanding, expert, connoisseur)

*Jonathan, uncle of David, is described as a man of discerning, I
Chron. 27:32*

A rebuke goes into a *discerning* one
more than 100 blows into a fool.
— Prov. 17:10

With the face of the *discerning* is wisdom,
— Prov. 17:24a

(From King Hezekiah's scribes)
And by a *discerning* person,
Who knoweth right — it is prolonged.
— Prov. 28:2

Whoso is keeping the law is a *discerning* son,
— Prov. 28:7

A rich man (אִישׁ ish) is wise in his own eyes,
 And the *discerning* poor searcheth him (i.e., finds him out).
— Prov. 28:11

Discretion
        discretion, devising, plotting מְזִמָּה (mezimmah) (modern:
scheme, plot, design)

This is an example of a Hebrew word used in two quite different ways – discretion, which is a positive trait, and plotting or scheming, which has a negative connotation. "Through the pride of the wicked, Is the poor inflamed, They are caught in devices that they devised," Psalms 10:2, is an example of the latter. On the other hand, Jer. 30:24 speaks of the "devices of his (the Lord's) heart.

Discretion shall keep you,
understanding shall watch over you.
—　　Prov. 2:11

My son, let not *discretion* and sound wisdom
depart from your eyes; keep them.
—　　Prov. 3:21

Keep *discretion* and may knowledge guard your lips.
—　　Prov. 5:2

I, wisdom, dwell in prudence,
and I find knowledge and *discretion*.
—　　Prov. 8:12

And whoso pursues *evil* — for his own death.
—　　Prov. 11:19

And one of wicked *devices* He condemneth.
—　　Prov. 12:2

The wicked have desired the net of *evil* doers,
—　　Prov. 12:12a

And a man (אִישׁ Yahweh) of wicked *devices* is hated.
—　　Prov. 14:17

The *evil* have bowed down before the good,
and the wicked at the gates of the righteous.
—   Prov. 14:19

Whoso is *devising* to do evil,
Him they call a master of wicked thoughts.
—   Prov. 24:8

taste, discretion, flavor טַעַם (ta'am) (modern: flavor, taste, reason, cause)

This word is one of the few for which the definition has changed somewhat during the years. It generally referred to tasting food.Manna had the taste of cake with honey, Ex. 16:31. Both Jonathan and David spoke of tasting food, I Sam. 1 and II Sam. 3. Yet, in its sngle appearance in Proverbs, it refers to discretion.

Like a gold ring in a hog's snout
is a beautiful woman without *taste*.
—   Prov. 11:22

Fear

fear, to be afraid, to revere יְרָאָה ('ra) (modern: far, to be afraid.)

This is another Hebrew word that has more than one use. Isaac "feared" to tell the men of Gerar that Rebecca was his wife, Gen. 26:6. On the other hand, there are frequent verses about the fear of the Lord.

Prov. 1:7, See Introduction

That they hated knowledge and chose not the fear of the Lord.
—   Prov. 1:29

My son, if you receive my words and hide my commandments with you

....

then you will understand the *fear* of the Lord (יְרְאָה Yahweh) and find the knowledge of God (אֱלֹהִים Elohim).
— 	Prov. 2:1, 5

Do not be wise in your own eyes,
fear the Lord (יהוה Yahweh) and depart from evil.
— 	Prov. 3:7

The *fear* of the Lord (יהוה Yahweh) is the hatred of evil.
— 	Prov. 8:13

The *fear* of the Lord (יהוה Yahweh) is the beginning of wisdom,
— 	Prov. 9:10

What is *feared* by the wicked shall come upon him,
— 	Prov. 10:24

The *fear* of the Lord (יהוה Yahweh) prolongs life
— 	Prov. 10:27

One walking in his uprightness is *fearing* the Lord (יהוה Yahweh),
— 	Prov. 14:2

The wise is *fearing* and turning from evil,
— 	Prov. 14:16

In *fear* of the Lord (יהוה Yahweh) one has strong confidence,
and to his sons shall be a hiding place.
The *fear* of the Lord (יהוה Yahweh)is a fountain of life,
that one may avoid the snares of death.
— 	Prov. 14:26-27

Better is a little with the *fear* of the Lord (יהוה Yahweh).
—   Prov. 15:16a

The *fear* of the Lord (יהוה Yahweh) is discipline in wisdom,
—   Prov. 15:33a

and by the *fear* of the Lord (יהוה Yahweh) one turns from evil.
—   Prov. 16:6b

The *fear* of the Lord (יהוה Yahweh) leads to life,
and he who has it rests satisfied,
he will not be visited with evil.
—   Prov. 19:23

The reward of humility is *fear* of the Lord (יהוה Yahweh),
riches and honor and life.
—   Prov. 22:4

continue in the *fear* of the Lord (יהוה Yahweh) all day.
—   Prov. 23:17

Fear the Lord (יהוה Yahweh), my son, and the king,
and do not associate with those who change.
—   Prov. 24:21

(From King Hezekiah's scribes)
The *fear* of a person (אָדָם adam) lays a snare,
but he who trusts in the Lord (יהוה Yahweh) is safe.
—   Prov. 29:25

(From King Lemuel of Massa)
but a woman who *fears* the Lord (יהוה Yahweh) is to be praised.
—   Prov. 31:30b

fear, dread, anxious פַּחַד (pakhad) (modern: fear, fright, awe)

Moses said the Lord God would lay dread upon tlose opposing the Israelites as they took the Promised Land, and no man would stand against them, Deut. 1:25.

In your calamity I will laugh,
I will mock when your *dread* comes.
when your *dread* and your calamity arrive like a tempest,
when distress and constraint come upon you.
— Prov. 1:26-27 (Wisdom is speaking.)

But the one listening to me shall dwell securely
and shall be at ease from the *dread* of evil.
— Prov. 1:33

Do not be afraid of sudden *dread* (i.e. panic),
— Prov. 3:25

(From King Hezekiah's scribes)
Blessed is the person (אָדָם adam) always *fearing* (God implied),
but he that hardeneth his heart will fall into calamity.
— Prov. 28:14

Glory

Exalt (wisdom) and she will lift you up,
she will honor you when you embrace her.
She shall give to your head a wreath of grace
with a crown of glory she will shield you.
— Prov. 4:8-9

glory, ornament, beauty, finery פְּאֵרַת (po'arah) (modern: pomp, glory, splendor, magnificenc)

123

The Hebrew word appears to apply to both physical beauty as well as character. Note in 17:6 and 20:29 that זָקֵן (zachen) can also be translated in the gender-neutral in both biblical and modern Hebrew as aged or the old, not merely as old man, and similarly, בָּחוּר (bachur) as well s young men.

A crown of *glory* is gray hair
in the way of righteousness it is found.
—   Prov. 16:31

The crown of the aged is their grandchildren,
and the *glory* of sons is their fathers.
—   Prov. 17:6

A person's (אָדָם adam) discretion makes his anger slow,
and it is his *glory* to overlook a sin.
—   Prov. 19:11b

The *glory* of youth is their vigor,
and the honor of the aged is their gray hair.
—   Prov. 20:29

(From King Hezekiah's scribes)
When the righteous rejoice, great is the *glory*,
—   Prov. 28:12

> honor, respect, reverence כָּבוֹד (kavod) (modern: dignity, hoinor, respect)

The sons of Laban accused Jacob of taking all that was their father's and gaining "all this honor," Gen. 31:1. Joseph told his brothers to inform their father of the honor he had received in Egypt, Gen. 45:13.

Honor the Lord (יהוה Yahweh) from your substance and from the first-fruits of all your produce.
—   Prov. 3:9

Length of days *is* in her right hand,
In her left *are* wealth and *honor*.
—   Prov. 3:16 (The reference is to Wisdom)

The wise shall inherit *honor,*
—   Prov. 3:35

Riches and *honor* are with me (wisdom),
enduring wealth and righteousness.
—   Prov. 8:18

A gracious woman holds to *honor*,
—   Prov. 11:16a

and before *honor* is humility.
—   Prov. 15:33b, 18:12b

It is an *honor* for a man (אִישׁ ish) to keep from strife,
—   Prov. 20:3

One who pursues righteousness and mercy
finds life, righteousness and *honor.*
—   Prov. 21:21

The reward of humility is fear of the Lord (יהוה Yahweh),
riches and *honor* and life.
—   Prov. 22:4

(From King Hezekiah's scribes)
The *honor* of God (אֱלֹהִים Elohim) is to conceal a matter,
—   Prov. 25:2

and to search out their *honor* is honor.
—   Prov. 25:27

Like snow in summer and like rain at harvest,
so *honor* is not right for a fool.
—   Prov. 26:1

As one who binds a stone in a sling,
so is he who gives *honor* to a fool.
—   Prov. 26:8

A person's (אָדָם adam) pride brings him low,
but the humble of spirit takes hold of honor.
—   Prov. 29:23

   ornament, splendor, honor הֲדָרָה (hadarah) (modern: adorn,
   glorify)

*I and II Chronicles and the Psalms, this Hebrew word is used to
glorify the Lord. Here, it lifts up people as the glory of the king, a
decidedly democratic notion.*

 In a multitude of people is *splendor* of the king,
—   Prov. 14:28

 Straight, level, even מֵישָׁר (mesharim) (modern: plain, level)

*See also "Honesty" in Chapter VII: Economic Matters. The
psalmist says the Lord judgs people evenly, 9:8.*

For receiving the instruction of wisdom, righteousness, judgment,
and *evenness*,
—   Prov. 1:3

Then you will understand righteousness and justice and *evenness*,
every good path;
for wisdom will come into your heart,
and knowledge will be pleasant to your soul;
discretion will watch over you;
—   Prov. 2:9-10

also:

(From King Hezekiah's scribes)
He who shares with a thief hates his soul;
he hears an oath but does not tell it.
—   Prov. 29:24

Humble, lowly, meek עֲנָוָה ('anavah) (modern: humble, modest)

In a prayer, David says the Lord's humility had made him great, II Sam. 22:36.

If he is scornful at the scorners,
yet to the *humble* he gives grace.
—   Prov. 3:34

before honor is *humility.*
—   Prov. 15:33b

Before destruction a man's (שֵׁבֶר ish) heart is haughty,
but before honor goes *humility.*
—   Prov. 18:12

The reward of *humility* is fear of the Lord (יהוה Yahweh),
riches and honor and life.
—   Prov. 22:4

Integrity, blameless, wholeness תָּמִים (tamim) (modern: innocent, simple, naïve, honest)

David professed to have integrity, II Sam. 22:24. The Lord acknowledged this, and admonished Solomon also to walk in integrity, I Kings 9:4.

(The Lord is) a shield for those walking with *integrity.*
—   Prov. 2:7

For the upright will inhabit the land,
and the (ones of) *integrity* will remain in it;
—   Prov. 2:21

One who walks in *integrity* walks safely,
—   Prov. 10:9a

The *integrity* of the upright guides them,
—   Prov. 11:3

The righteousness of (those with) *integrity* maketh right his way,
—   Prov. 11:5a

but his delight are those of *integrity*.
—   Prov. 11:20b

Righteousness keepeth him who has *integrity* in the way,
—   Prov. 13:6a

Better is the poor who walks in his *integrity*
than one who is crooked in speech and he is a fool.
—   Prov. 19:1

The righteous walks about in his *integrity*
—   Prov. 20:7

(From King Hezekiah's scribes)
Better is the poor who walks in his *integrity*
than one who is crooked two ways even if he is rich.
—   Prov. 28:6

One who walks in *integrity* will be delivered,
but one who is crooked in his two ways will fall at once.
—   Prov. 28:18

Those of blood hate one who has *integrity*,
and the upright seek his life.
—   Prov. 29:10

Learning, instruction לֶקַח (leqakh) (modern: lesson)

Beware of confusing this Hebrew word with another variation of the word that is a form of the verb to take. Of all the uses of this word, only Proverbs and Isaiah 29:24 use it with the definition of learning.

The wise does hear and increase *learning*,
—   Prov. 1:5a

For good *learning* I have given to you,
—   Prov. 4:2a

Teach a righteous man and he will add *learning*.
—   Prov. 9:9

The wise of heart makes prudent his mouth,
and sweetness of lips adds *learning*.
—   Prov. 16:21

The heart of the wise makes prudent his mouth,
and on his lips he adds *learning*.
—   Prov. 16:23

Practical wisdom תּוּשִׁיָּה (tushiyyah) (modern: pesence of mind, resource, wisdom)

Compare wise guidance, (thchbol). The prophet Micah says it is practical wisdom to fear the Lord's name, Micah 6:9.

To me is counsel and *practical wisdom,*
To me is understanding, in me is strength.
— Prov. 8:14

One who separates himself (is estranged)
seeks to break out against all *practical wisdom.*
— Prov. 18:1

Prudence

Three words are used in the Hebrew Bible that have been translated as "prudence." Perhaps the most interesting is עָרְמָה *('ormah), which has the connotation of shrewdness and astuteness; see Prov. 22:3.*

>   astute, cunning, crafty עָרְמָה ('ormah) (modern: crafty, sly, cunning)

The men of Gibeon used astuteness to try to thwart the advance of the Israelites by arranging a phony alliance, Josh. 9.

O simple ones, learn, *astuteness.*
— Prov. 8:5a

I, wisdom, dwell in *astuteness,*
and I find knowledge and discretion.
— Prov. 8:12

but shame, the *astute* cover.
— Prov. 12:16b

An *astute* person (אָדָם adam) covers knowledge,
but the fools of heart call out folly.
— Prov. 12:23

Every astute one deals with knowledge,
— Prov. 13:16a

The wisdom of the *astute* discerns his way,
— Prov. 14:8a

the *astute* watches his step.
— Prov. 14:15b

but the *astute* are circled with knowledge.
— Prov. 14:18b

A fool despises his father's discipline,
but the one heeding correction is *astute*.
— Prov. 15:5

A servant who acts from *astuteness* will rule over a son who acts
shamefully,
 and among the brothers he will share the inheritance.
— Prov. 17:2

Strike a scoffer, but the simple will be *astute*.
— Prov. 19:25a

An *astute* one sees evil and hides himself,
but the simple pass on and are punished.
— Prov. 22:3, 27:12

    wise, skillful מַשְׂכִּיל (maskil) (modern: scholar,
intellectual, learned)

*David acted wisely, a trait Saul noticed, I Sam. 18:14-15. Notice
the similarity between* מַשְׂכִּיל *and* שֵׂכֶל

but one who restrains his lips is *wise*
— Prov. 10:19b

The path of life is upward to the *wise*
that he may avoid hell beneath.
— Prov. 15:24

He who acts from *prudence* on a matter will find good,
—   Prov. 16:20a

A servant who acts from *prudence*
will rule over a son who acts shamefully,
and among the brothers he will share the inheritance.
—   Prov. 17:2

and from the Lord (יהוה Yahweh) is a wife who acts from prudence.
—   Prov. 19:14b

    <u>good sense, insight</u> שֵׂכֶל (sehhel) (modern: brains, intellect, intelligence, wisdom)

King Hiram of Tyre praised Solomon as a person of good sense and discretion, II Chron. 2:12. Abigail was said to have good sense, I Sam. 25:3.

By his *good sense* a man (אִישׁ ish) shall be praised
—   Prov. 12:8a

good sense gives grace.
—   Prov. 13:15a

A well of life is *good sense* to its owners,
—   Prov. 16:22a

A bribe is a stone of grace in the eyes of its owner,
wherever he turns, he has *good sense.*
—   Prov. 17:8

A person's (אָדָם adam) *good sense* slows his anger,
—   Prov. 19:11a

A person (אָדָם adam) who wanders out of the way of *good sense* shall rest in the assembly of the dead.
—   Prov. 21:16

Pure

Almost always in the Hebrew Bible the word pure is used to describe elements of the Tabernacle and Temple, rather than a person. This may demonstrate how rare a person of purity is. There are two related Hebrew words; notice that Prov. 20:9 uses both.

     pure, clean   זַךְ (zakh) (modern: pure, transparent)

All the ways of a man (אִישׁ ish) are pure in his own eyes,
—   Prov. 16:2a

Who can say, I have *purified* my heart,
I am clean from sin.
—   Prov. 20:9

Even a child makes himself known by his acts,
whether what he does is *pure* and upright.
—   Prov. 20:11

but the work of the *pure* is upright.
—   Prov. 21:8b

     purity, clean   טָהוֹר (tahor) (modern: purify, purge)

Throughout other parts of the Hebrew Bible this word is used to signify clean animals or clean objects and pure gold and the like.

but *purifying* are the words of pleasantness.
—   Prov. 15:26

Who can say, I have purified my heart,

I am *clean* from sin.
— Prov. 20:9

One who loves *purity* of heart ... will have the king as his friend.
— Prov. 22:11

(From Agur of Massa)
A generation *pure* in its own eyes,
(yet) from its own filth not washed.
— Prov. 30:12

Righteous צַדִּיק (tsaddiq) (modern: just, righteous, pious, virtuous)

The Lord saved Noah and his household because they were righteous, Gen.. 7:1, and Judah said his widowed daughter-in-law, Tamar, with whom he had unwittingly slept, was more righteous than he, because he, Judah, had not given her to his other son, Gen. 38:26.

Then you will understand *righteousness* and justice and equity,
every good path;
for wisdom will come into your heart,
and knowledge will be pleasant to your soul;
— Prov. 2:9-10

So you will walk in the way of good men
and keep to the paths of the *righteous.*
— Prov. 2:20

The Lord's curse is on the house of the wicked,
but he blesses the abode of the *righteous.*
— Prov. 3:33

But the path of the *righteous* is like the light of dawn,
which shines brighter and brighter until full day.
— Prov. 4:18

All the words of my mouth are *righteous;*
there is nothing twisted or crooked in them.
—   Prov. 8:8 (Wisdom is speaking.)

By me kings reign,
and rulers decree what is *righteous;*
by me princes rule,
and nobles govern the earth.
—   Prov. 8:15-16

Riches and honor (are) with me,
enduring wealth and *righteousness.*
—   Prov. 8:18

I walk in the way of *righteousness,*
in the paths of justice,
endowing with wealth those who love me,
and filling their treasuries.
—   Prov. 8:20-21 (Wisdom is speaking.)

but *righteousness* delivers from death.
The Lord does not let the *righteous* go hungry,
—   Prov. 10:2b and Prov. 10:3a

Blessings are on the head of the *righteous,*
—   Prov. 10:6a

The memory of the *righteous* is a blessing,
—   Prov. 10:7a

The mouth of the *righteous* is a fountain of life,
—   Prov. 10:11a

The wage of the *righteous* leads to life,
—   Prov. 10:16a

The tongue of the *righteous* is choice silver,
—   Prov. 10:20a

The lips of the *righteous* feed many,
—   Prov. 10:21a

What the wicked dreads will come upon him,
but the desire of the *righteous* will be granted.
When the tempest passes, the wicked is no more,
but the righteous is established for ever.
—   Prov. 10:24-25

The hope of the *righteous* ends in gladness,

but the expectation of the wicked comes to naught.
The Lord is a stronghold to him whose way is upright,
but destruction to evildoers.
The *righteous* will never be removed,
but the wicked will not dwell in the land.
The mouth of the *righteous* brings forth wisdom,
but the perverse tongue will be cutoff.
The lips of the *righteous* know what is acceptable,
but the mouth of the wicked, what is perverse.
—   Prov. 10:28-32

but *righteousness* delivers from death.
The *righteousness* of the blameless keeps his way straight,
but the wicked falls down by his own wickedness.
The *righteousness* of the upright delivers them,
but the treacherous are taken captive by their lust.
When the wicked dies, his hope perishes,
and the expectation of the godless comes to nought.
The *righteous* is delivered from trouble,
and the wicked gets into it instead.
With his mouth the godless man would destroy his neighbor,
but by knowledge the *righteous* are delivered.
When it goes well with the *righteous*,

the city rejoices,
and when the wicked perish there are shouts of gladness.
By the blessing of the upright a city is exalted,
but is overthrown by the mouth of the wicked.
—   Prov. 11:4b-11

but one who sows *righteousness* gets a true reward.
He who is steadfast in righteousness will live,
—   Prov. 11:18b-19a

but those who are *righteous* will be delivered.
—   Prov. 11:21

The desire of the *righteous* ends only in good,
—   Prov. 11:23a

but like a green lead the *righteous* will flourish
—   Prov. 11:28b

The fruit of *righteousness* is a tree of life,
—   Prov. 11:30a

If the *righteous* is repaid on earth,
indeed, also the wicked and sinner.
—   Prov. 11:31

but the root of the *righteous* will never be moved.
—   Prov. 12:3b

The thoughts of the *righteous* are just;
—   Prov. 12:5a

but the house of the *righteous* will stand.
—   Prov. 12:7b

A *righteous* one regards the life of his beast,
—   Prov. 12:10

but the root of the *righteous* yields (fruit).
—   Prov. 12:12b

but the *righteous* escapes from trouble.
—   Prov. 12:13b

One who breathes truth reveals *righteousness,*
—   Prov. 12:17

No evil befalls the *righteous,*
—   Prov. 12:21a

A *righteous* one turns away evil,
—   Prov. 12:26a

In the path of *righteousness* is life,
—   Prov. 12:28a

The *righteous* hates falsehood ...
Righteousness guards the way of the perfect,
—   Prov. 13:5a, 6a

The light of the *righteous* rejoices,
—   Prov. 13:9a

but the *righteous* shall be rewarded with good.
—   Prov. 13:21b

but the sinner's wealth is laid up for the *righteous.*
—   Prov. 13:22a

The *righteous* eats to his soul's satisfaction,
—   Prov. 13:25a

the wicked (bow down) at the gates of the *righteous.*
—   Prov. 14:19b
but the *righteous* finds refuge in his death.

—   Prov. 14:32b

Righteousness exalts a nation,
—   Prov. 14:34a

In the house of the *righteous* is much treasure,
—   Prov. 15:6a

but he (the Lord) (יהוה Yahweh) loves the one pursuing
righteousness.
—   Prov. 15:9b

The heart of the *righteous* ponders how to answer,
—   Prov. 15:28a

but (the Lord) (יהוה Yahweh) hears the prayer of the *righteous.*
—   Prov. 15:29b

Better is a little with *righteousness*
than much increase without justice.
—   Prov. 16:8

It is an abomination to kings to commit wickedness,
for the throne is established by I
—   Prov. 16:12

The delight of kings are *righteous* lips,
—   Prov. 16:13

Gray hair is a crown of glory,
it is gained in a *righteous* life.
—   Prov. 16:31

He who makes *righteous* the wicked and condemns the righteous,
are both alike an abomination to the Lord.
—   Prov. 17:15

To impose a fine on the *righteous* is not good,
—   Prov. 17:26a

or (it is not good) to deprive a *righteous* man of justice.
—   Prov. 18:5b

The name of the Lord (יהוה Yahweh) is a strong tower,
the *righteous* runs into it and is safe.
—   Prov. 18:10

The first (to state his case) seems *right,*
until his neighbor comes and tests him.
—   Prov. 18:17

The *righteous* walks about in his integrity—
blessed are his sons after him.
—   Prov. 20:7

To do *righteousness* and justice
is more acceptable to the Lord (יהוה Yahweh) than sacrifice.
—   Prov. 21:3

The *righteous* one wisely considers the house of the wicked,
He overturns the wicked for evil.
—   Prov. 21:12

When justice is done, it is a joy to the *righteous*
but dismay to the workers of evil.
—   Prov. 21:15

The wicked is a ransom for the *righteous,*
—   Prov. 21:18a

He who pursues *righteousness* and mercy
will find life, *righteousness* and honor.
—   Prov. 21:21

All day long he lusts with lust,
but the *righteous* gives and withholds not.
—   Prov. 21:26

The father of the *righteous* will greatly rejoice;
he who begats a wise son will be glad in him.
Let your father and mother be glad,
let her who bore you rejoice.
—   Prov. 23:24-25

Lie not in ambush as a wicked one at the abode of the *righteous,*
do not violate his home;
for a righteous one falls seven times, and rises again;
but the wicked shall stumble into evil.
—   Prov. 24:15-16

(From King Hezekiah's scribes)
Take away the wicked from the presence of the king,
and his throne shall be established in *righteousness.*
—   Prov. 25:5

Like a fouled spring or a polluted fountain
is the *righteous* tottering before the wicked.
—   Prov. 25:26

The wicked flee when no one is pursuing,
but the *righteous* are as bold as a lion.
—   Prov. 28:1

When the *righteous* rejoice great is the glory,
but when the wicked rise a man (adam) will be sought.
—   Prov. 28:12

When the wicked rise, a person (אָדָם adam) hides himself,
but when they perish, the *righteous* multiply.
—   Prov. 28:28

When the *righteous* increase, the people rejoice;
but when the wicked rule, the people groan.
— Prov. 29:2

but a *righteous* one sings and rejoices.
The *righteous* knows the plea of the poor;
— Prov. 29:6b-7a

When the wicked multiply, sin increases;
but the *righteous* shall see their fall.
— Prov. 29:16

An abomination to the *righteous* is an unjust man,
and an abomination to the wicked is the way of the upright.
— Prov. 29:27

(From King Lemuel of Massa)
Open your mouth, judge *righteously*,
and defend the poor and the needy.
— Prov. 31:9

Satisfied, to be full שׂבע (sava) (modern: to be satisfied, satiated, eat enough)

Abaham was "full of years," Gen. 25:8. Note, however, how many verses refer to food.

He who serves his land will be *satisfied* with bread,
— Prov. 12:11a

From fruit of a man's mouth (ish) he is *satisfied* with good,
— Prov. 12:14a

From his own ways the heart of the backslider will be *satisfied*,
— Prov. 14:14

From fruit of a man's mouth his belly shall be *satisfied*,
— Prov. 18:20

The fear of the Lord (יהוה Yahweh) leads to life,
and he who has it rests *satisfied*,
he will not be visited with evil.
— Prov. 19:23

Do not love sleep, lest you be dispossessed,
open your eyes, be *satisfied* with bread.
— Prov. 20:13

(From King Hezekiah's scribes)
Sheol and destruction are not (never) *satisfied*,
the eyes of a person (אָדָם adam) are not satisfied.
— Prov. 27:20

(From Agur of Massa)
There are three things that are never *satisfied*, yea, four
— Prov. 30:15b

Understanding
        understanding, reason, intelligence תְּבוּנָה (tevunah)
(modern: intelligence, reason, understanding, wisdom)

God gave Solomon understanding and reason, I Kings 5:9. King Hiram of Tyre, the master builder, had understanding and reason, I Kings 7:14.

My son, if you receive my words and treasure up my commandments with you, making your ear attentive to wisdom and inclining your heart to *understanding;*
yes, if you cry out for insight and raise your voice for *understanding,*

if you seek it like silver and search for it as hidden treasures;

then you will understand the fear of the Lord (יהוה Yahweh) and
find the knowledge of God (אֱלֹהִים Elohim).
For the Lord (יהוה Yahweh) gives wisdom;
and from his mouth comes knowledge and *understanding;*
he stores up sound wisdom for the upright;
he is a shield to those who walk in integrity,
guarding the paths of justice and preserving the way of his saints,
—   Prov. 2:1-8

for wisdom will come into your heart,
and knowledge will be pleasant to your soul;
discretion will watch over you;
understanding will guard you;
delivering you from the way of evil,
from men of perverted speech,
who forsake the paths of uprightness to walk in the ways of
darkness,
who rejoice in doing evil and delight in the perverseness of evil;
men who paths are crooked,
and who are devious in their ways.
—   Prov. 2:10-15

Happy is the person (אָדָם adam) who finds wisdom,
and the man who gets *understanding,*
for the gain from it is better than gain from silver
and its profit better than gold.
She is more precious than jewels,
and nothing you desire can compare with her.
Long life is in her right hand;
in her left hand are riches and honor.
Her ways are ways of pleasantness,
and all her paths are peace.
She is a tree of life to those who lay hold of her;
those who hold her fast are called happy.
The Lord (יהוה Yahweh) by wisdom founded the earth;
by *understanding* he established the heavens;

by his knowledge the deeps broke forth,
and the clouds drop down the dew.
—   Prov. 3:13-20

My son, be attentive to my wisdom,
incline your ear to my *understanding*;
that you may keep discretion,
and your lips may guard knowledge.
—   Prov. 5:1-2

And does not wisdom call?
and *understanding* give her voice?
—   Prov. 8:1

but wise conduct is pleasure to a man (אִישׁ ish) of *understanding*.
—   Prov. 10:23b

but a man (אִישׁ ish) of understanding remains silent.
—   Prov. 11:12

He who is slow to anger has great *understanding*,
—   Prov. 14:29a

but a man (אִישׁ ish) of *understanding* walks upright.
—   Prov. 15:21b

and he who has a cool spirit is a man (אִישׁ ish) of *understanding*.
—   Prov. 17:27b

A fool takes no pleasure in *understanding*,
but only in expressing his opinion.
—   Prov. 18:2

he who keeps *understanding* will find good.
—   Prov. 19:8

Like deep water is counsel in a man's (אִישׁ ish) heart,

but as man (אִישׁ ish) of *understanding* will draw it out.
— Prov. 20:5

There is no wisdom, no *understanding*, no counsel against the Lord
(יהוה Yahweh).
— Prov. 21:30

By wisdom a house is built, and by *understanding* it is established;
by knowledge the rooms are filled with all precious and pleasant
riches.....
A virile man (גֶּבֶר gbr) (or warrior) is wise in strength,
a man (אִישׁ ish) of knowledge firms up strength;
for by wise guidance you can wage your war,
and in abundance of counselors there is victory.
Wisdom is too high for a fool;
in the gate he does not open mouth.
— Prov. 24:3-7

(From King Hezekiah's scribes)
A ruler lacking *understanding* evens adds oppression,
— Prov. 28:16

   understanding, discernment, perception בִּין (binah)
(modern: wisdom, intellect)

King Huram of Tyre said David had perception, II Chron. 2:11-12.

Trust in the Lord with all your heart,
and do not rely on your *perception*.
— Prov. 3:5

Hear, O sons, a father's instruction,
and be attentive, that you may obtain *perception*
for I give you good precepts:
do not forsake my teaching.
When I was a son with my father, tender,

the only one in the sight of my mother,
he taught me, and said to me,
"Let your heart hold fast my words,
and keep my commandments, and live;
do not forget, and do not turn away from the words of my mouth.
Get wisdom, get *perception*.
Do not forsake her, and she will keep you;
love her, and she will guard you.
The beginning of wisdom is this:
Get wisdom, and whatever you get, get *perception*.
Prize her highly, and she will exalt you;
she will honor you if you embrace her;
she will bestow on you a beautiful crown."
—   Prov. 4:1-9

Say to wisdom, "You are my sister,"
and call *perception* your intimate friend.
—   Prov. 7:4

Simple-minded ones, *perceive* wisdom,
and dullards, be of a *perceptive* heart.
—   Prov. 8:5

I have counsel and practical wisdom,
I have *perception*, I have strength.
—   Prov. 8:14

Forsake the simple and live and walk in the way of *perception*.
—   Prov. 9:6

and the knowledge of the Holy Ones is *perceptive*.
—   Prov. 9:10

On the lips of him who has *perception* wisdom is found,
—   Prov. 10:13a

but knowledge is easy for the one of *perception.*
— Prov. 14:6b

to get *perception* is to be chosen rather than silver.
— Prov. 16:16b

Even a fool who keeps silent is considered wise,
when he closes his lips, he is thought (to be) *perceptive.*
— Prov. 17:28

and correct one with *perception*, he will *perceive* knowledge.
— Prov. 19:25b

Work not to be rich, and from your own *perception* cease.
— Prov. 23:4

Buy truth, and do not sell it;
buy wisdom, instruction, and *perception.*
— Prov. 23:23

(From King Hezekiah's scribes)
A rich man (אִישׁ ish) is wise in his own eyes,
but a poor man who has *perception* will find him out.
— Prov. 28:11

(From Agur of Massa)
Surely I am more brutish than any (אִישׁ ish),
and am not a person (אָדָם adam) of *perception.*
I have not learned wisdom and I do not have the knowledge of
holiness.
— Prov. 30:2-3

Upright, integrity יָשָׁר (yashar) (modern: straight, direct, honest, candid)

Achish, the leader of the Philistines, said that David was upright, I Sam. 29:6. Saul initially thought the relationship between his daughter Michal and David was upright, I Sam. 18: 20, 26. David himself claimed to be upright in heart, I Chron. 29:17.

For the *upright* will inhabit the land,
and men of integrity will remain in it;
—   Prov. 2:21

for the perverse man is an abomination to the Lord,
but the *upright* are in his confidence.
—   Prov. 3:32

I have taught you the way of wisdom;
I have led you in the paths of *uprightness.*
—   Prov. 4:11

Hear, for I will speak excellent things,
and from the opening of my lips, *upright* things.
—   Prov. 8:6

All of them are plain to the discerning,
and *upright* to those finding knowledge.
—   Prov. 8:9

(A foolish woman) calls those passing on their way,
going *upright* on their paths.
—   Prov. 9:15

The integrity of the *upright* guides them,
—   Prov. 11:3a

The righteousness of the *upright* delivers them,
—   Prov. 11:6a

By the blessing of the *upright* a city is lifted up,
—   Prov. 11:11

but the mouth of the *upright* delivers them.
—   Prov. 12:6b

A dullard is *upright* in his own eyes,
—   Prov. 12:15

One who walks in *uprightness* fears the Lord (יהוה Yahweh),
—   Prov. 14:2a

but among the *upright,* (there is) favor.
—   Prov. 14:9a

but the tent of the *upright* will flourish.
—   Prov. 14:11b

There is a way (seeming) *upright* to a man,
but its end is the ways of death.
—   Prov. 14:12

but the prayer of the *upright* is his (the Lord's) delight.
—   Prov. 15:8b

but the path of the *upright* is plain.
—   Prov. 15:19b

but a man (אִישׁ ish) of understanding walks *upright.*
—   Prov. 15:21b

Righteous lips are the delight of kings,
and he loves him who speaks *uprightly.*
—   Prov. 16:13

The way of the *upright* turns aside from evil,
he who guards his way preserveth his soul.
—   Prov. 16:17

There is a way which seems *upright* to a man,
but its end is the way to death.
—   Prov. 16:25

and to strike nobles for *uprightness* is not good.
—   Prov. 17:26b

Even a child makes himself known by his acts,
whether what he does is pure and *upright*.
—   Prov. 20:11

Every way of a man (אִישׁ ish) is *upright* in his eyes,
but the Lord (יהוה Yahweh) weighs the heart.
—   Prov. 21:2

but the conduct of the pure is *upright*.
—   Prov. 21:8b

and the betrayer (is a ransom) for the *upright*.
—   Prov. 21:18b

A wicked man (ish) hardens his face,
but the upright establishes his way.
—   Prov. 21:29

My soul will rejoice when your lips speak what is *upright*.
—   Prov. 23:16

(From King Hezekiah's scribes)
The one leading the *upright* into an evil way will fall into his own pit;
but the blameless will have a goodly inheritance.
—   Prov. 28:10

Men (שׁיאֵ ish) of blood hate the blameless,
but the *upright* seek his soul.
— Prov. 29:10

Hateful to the righteous is an unjust man (שׁיאֵ ish),
and hateful to the wicked is the way of the *upright*.
— Prov. 29:27

Chapter 5: UNGODLY TRAITS

<u>Abomination, horrible deed</u> תּוֹעֵבָה (to'evah) (modern: abhorrence, abomnation, ugly act)

The enslaved Israelites were an abomination to the Egyptians, Gen. 43 and 46. In II Chron. 34:33, good King Josiah removed the abominations and made the Israelites serve the Lord. This is the word applied in Lev. 18:22-30 to homosexual behavior. Deuteronomy lists other abominations — graven images, 7:25; burning children for other gods, 12:31; soothsayers, sorcerers, wizards and necromaniacs, 18:11-12; dressing in drag, 22:5; and, if none of these things fits you, giving false weights or measurements, in short, "anyone doing injustice/unrighteousness," 25:16. Note how frequently the abominations are "to the Lord."

For the devious is an *abomination* to the Lord (יהוה Yahweh),
—   Prov. 3:32

These six things the Lord (יהוה Yahweh) hates,
and seven are an *abomination* to his soul.
Eyes high — tongues false — and hands shedding innocent blood —

heart devising thoughts of vanity — feet hasting to run to evil —
A false witness breathes out lies –
And one sending forth contentions between brethren.
—   Prov. 6:16-19

and an *abomination* to my lips is wickedness.
—   Prov. 8:7

153

False balances are an *abomination* to the Lord (יהוה Yahweh).
— Prov. 11:1

An *abomination* to the Lord (יהוה Yahweh) are the perverse of heart,
— Prov. 11:20

An *abomination* to the Lord (יהוה Yahweh) are lips of falsehood.
— Prov. 12:22

it is an *abomination* to fools to depart from evil.
— Prov. 13:19b

The sacrifice of the wicked is an *abomination* to the Lord (יהוה Yahweh...
The way of the wicked is an *abomination* to the Lord (יהוה Yahweh).
— Prov. 15:8a, 9a

An *abomination* to the Lord (יהוה Yahweh) are the thoughts of the evil,
— Prov. 15:26a

Every one who is haughty in heart is an *abomination* to the Lord (יהוה Yahweh),
be assured, he will not go unpunished.
— Prov. 16:5

It is an *abomination* to kings to commit wickedness,
for the throne is established by righteousness.
— Prov. 16:12

He who makes righteous the wicked and condemns the righteous,
are both alike an *abomination* to the Lord.
— Prov. 17:15

Diverse weights and diverse measures are both alike an
abomination onto the Lord.
—   Prov. 20:10

An *abomination* to the Lord are diverse weights,
and deceitful scales are not good.
—   Prov. 20:23

The sacrifice of the wicked is an *abomination*,
how much more when he brings with it evil intent.
—   Prov. 21:27

and an *abomination* to persons (אָדָם adam) is a scoffer.
—   Prov. 24:9b

(From King Hezekiah's scribes)
By his lips does a hater dissemble,
and in his heart he places deceit,
when his voice is gracious trust not in him,
for seven *abominations* are in his heart.
—   Prov. 26:24-25

If one turns away his ear from hearing the law,
even his prayer is an *abomination*.
—   Prov. 28:9

An *abomination* to the righteous is an unjust man (אִישׁ ish),
and an *abomination* to the wicked is the way of the upright.
—   Prov. 29:27

Backslider סוּג (sug) (modern: the word does not appear)

*This Hebrew word also was used in a couple of ways. In Deut.
26:25 and 27:17 it refers to moving a neighbor's fence or border.
In Proverbs, it also refers to one's behavior.*

With the fruit of his ways the *backslider* will be filled,
— Prov. 14:14a

Remove not a border of olden times, that thy fathers have made.
— Prov. 22:28

Remove not a border of olden times, and into fields of the fatherless enter not,
— Prov. 23:10

Boorish, brutish, stupiḏ בַּעַר (ba'ar) (modern: ignoramus)

This word is almost identical to the Hebrew word for burn. It is used in this connection very frequently throughout the Hebrew Bible. As in the definition used in Proverbs, the prophet Isaiah said the wise counselors of Pharaoh had become boorish (19:11).)

but one hating correction is *boorish*.
— Prov. 12:1b

(From Agur of Massa)
Surely I am more *boorish* than any one,
— Prov. 30:2 *(Agur speaking self-depracatingly.)*

Cruel אַכְזָרִי (`akhzar) (modern: cruel, brutal)

The venom of an asp is cruel, Deut. 32:33 In his suffering, Job said God had turned cruel toward him, 30:21.

Lest you give yourself to others and your years to the *cruel* one.
— Prov. 5:9 *(Addressed to the son about contact with a strange woman.)*

but the *cruel* one hurts himself.
— Prov. 11:17b

but the mercies of the wicked are *cruel.*
—   Prov. 12:10b

A rebel seeks evil so a *cruel* messenger is sent against him.
—   Prov. 17:11

(From King Hezekiah's scribes)
Burning anger is *cruel.*
—   Prov. 27:4

Deceit

    <u>deceit, fraud</u> מִרְמָה (mirmah) (modern: deceit, fraud)

Esau told Isaac that Jacob had gone to him deceitfully. Jacob's sons answered Shechem the Hivite deceitfully because he had slept with their sister Dinah, Gen. 34:13.

Balances of *deceit* are an abomination to the Lord (יהוה Yahweh),
—   Prov. 11:1

the counsel of the wicked is *deceit.*
—   Prov. 12:5

but a witness of falsehoods (reveals) *deceit.*
—   Prov. 12:17

but the folly of fools is *deceit.*

Deceit is in the heart of those plotting evil.
—   Prov. 12:20a

but the folly of fools is *deceit.*
—   Prov. 14:8

but a *deceitful* (witness) utters lies.
—   Prov. 14:25

and *deceitful* scales are not good.
— Prov. 20:23b

(From King Hezekiah's scribes)
He who hates dissembles with his lips,
and he lays up *deceit*.
— Prov. 26:24

deceitful, treacherous בֹּגֵד (boged) (modern: betray)

There is a close similarity between this word and the Hebrew word for garment.

And the soul of the *treacherous* — violence.
— Prov. 13:2

But the way of *traitors* is continual,
— Prov. 13:15b

The eyes of the Lord keep watch over knowledge,
but he overthrows the words of the *treacherous*.
— Prov. 22:12

(From king Hezekiah's scribes)
Like a bad tooth and a slipping foot is trust in a *traitor* in a day of distress.
— Prov. 25:19

lie, falsehood, deceit שֶׁקֶר (sheqer) (modern: lie, untruth, fib)

We are not to give false testimony against our neighbor, Ex. 20: 16. The psalmist said every falsehood he hated, 119:128. See also "Truth and Lying" in Chapter XI: Principles.)

Whoevers covers hatred with *lying* lips,
and who brings out an evil report is a fool.
— Prov. 10:18

The wicked makes a *deceit* of wages,
—   Prov. 11:18

The lip of truth is established for ever,
and for a moment — a tongue of *falsehood*.
—   Prov. 12:19

An abomination to the Lord (יהוה Yahweh) are *lying* lips,
—   Prov. 12:22a

A *false* word the righteous hateth,
—   Prov. 13:5

And a false witness breatheth out *lies.*
—   Prov. 14:5

A *liar* listens to the tongue of (evil) desire.
—   Prov 17:4

Not comely for a fool is a lip of excellency,
Much less for a noble a lip of *falsehood.*
—   Prov. 17:7

Sweet to a man (אִישׁ ish) is the bread of *deceit,*
but afterwards his mouth will be filled with gravel.
—   Prov. 20:17

The making of treasures by a *lying* tongue,
a vanity driven away of those seeking death.
—   Prov. 21:6

(From King Hezekiah's scribes)
Clouds and wind, and rain there is none,
a man (אִישׁ ish) boasting himself in a *false* gift.
—   Prov. 25:14

A maul, and a sword, and a sharp arrow,
the man (אִישׁ ish) testifying against his neighbour a *false*
testimony.
—   Prov. 25:18

A *lying* tongue hates its bruised ones,
and a flattering mouth works an overthrow!
—   Prov. 26:28

A ruler who attends to *lying* words,
all his ministers are wicked.
—   Prov. 29:12

(From King Lemuel of Massa)
The grace is *deceitful* (i.e., charm can be deceitful)
—   Prov. 31:30a

Deceive, entice פתה (patah)hpth) (modern: seduce, tempt)

*Exodus uses this word in 22:15, "When a man entices a virgin who
is not betrothed. and has lain with her, he does certainly endow
her to himself for a wife."*

Do not ... *entice* with your lips.
—   Prov. 24:28b

Evil

evil, distress, adversity רַע (ra') (modern: bad, wicked, evil)

*The Lord saw that people were evil and decided to flood the earth,
Genesis 6:5. See also comments below on the next Hebrew word
for evil.*

... from the way of *evil*,
from men (אִישׁ ish) of perverted speech,

who forsake the paths of uprightness to walk in the ways of
darkness,
who rejoice in doing *evil* and delight in the perverseness of *evil*;
ones whose paths are crooked,
and who are devious in their ways.
—   Prov. 2:12-15

fear the Lord (יהוה Yahweh) and turn away from *evil*.
—   Prov. 3:7b

Do not plan *evil* against your neighbor,
who dwells trustingly beside you.
Do not strive with a person (אדם adam) for no reason,
when he has done you no *evil*.
—   Prov. 3:29-30

Do not enter the path of the wicked,
and do not walk in the way of *evil* ones.
Avoid it; do not go on it and pass on.
For they cannot sleep unless they have done wrong;
they are robbed of sleep unless they have made some one stumble.
For they eat the bread of wickedness and drink the wine of
violence.
—   Prov. 4:14-17

Do not swerve to the right or to the left;
turn your foot away from *evil*.
—   Prov. 4:26-27

A worthless person (אדם adam), an evil man (איש ish), goes
about with crooked speech,
winks with his eyes, scrapes with his feet, points with his finger,
with perverted heart devises *evil*, continually sowing discord,
therefore calamity will come upon him suddenly;
in a moment he will be broken beyond healing.
—   Prov. 6:12-15

There are six things which the Lord (היה Yahweh) hates,
seven which are an abomination to him:
haughty eyes, a lying tongue, and hands that shed innocent blood, a
heart that devises *evil* plans, feet that make haste to run to *evil*, a
false witness who breathes out lies, and one who sows discord
among brothers.
— Prov. 6:16-19

The fear of the Lord (יהוה Yahweh) is hatred of *evil*.
Pride and arrogance and the way of *evil* and perverted speech I
hate.
— Prov. 8:13

One suffers *evil* when he gives surety for a stranger,
— Prov. 11:14a

(Though joined) hand in hand, an *evil* one shall not be acquitted,
— Prov. 11:21a

but one pursuing *evil*, it will come to him.
— Prov. 11:27b

In the sin of the lips is the snare of *evil*,
— Prov. 12:13a

Deceit is in the heart of those plotting *evil*.
— Prov. 12:20a

but the wicked shall be filled with *evil*.
— Prov. 12:21b

but to turn away from *evil* is an abomination to fools.
— Prov. 13:19a

but the friend of fools suffers *evil*.
Sinners are pursued by *evil*,
— Prov. 13:20b-21a

The wise fears and turns from *evil*,
— Prov. 14:16a

Do they not err that devise *evil*?
— Prov. 14:22a

The wicked is overthrown through his *evil*-doing,
— Prov. 14:32a

The eyes of the Lord (יהוה Yahweh) are in every place,
keeping watch on the *evil* and the good.
— Prov. 15:3

Discipline is the path for the one forsaking *evil*,
— Prov. 15:10a

All the days of the afflicted are *evil*,
— Prov. 15:15a

An abomination to the Lord (יהוה Yahweh) are the thoughts of the
evil,
— Prov. 15:26a

but the mouth of the wicked pours out *evil* things.
— Prov. 15:28

and by the fear of the Lord (יהוה Yahweh) one turns from *evil*.
— Prov. 16:6b

The way of the upright turns aside from *evil*,
— Prov. 16:17a

A worthless man (אִישׁ ish) plots *evil*,
— Prov. 16:27a

He who shuts his eyes to plot to plan froward things,
pressing his lips, brings *evil* to pass.
— Prov. 16:30b

An *evil*-doer listens to troubling lips,
and a liar gives heed to a tongue of (evil) desire.
— Prov. 17:4

A rebel seeks *evil,* and so a cruel messenger will be sent against
him.
— Prov. 17:11

He who returns *evil* for good,
evil will not depart from his house.
— Prov. 17:13

and one perverse in his tongue falls into *evil*.
— Prov. 17:20b

The fear of the Lord (יהוה Yahweh) leads to life,
and he who has it rests satisfied,
he will not be visited with *evil*.
— Prov. 19:23

A king who sits on the throne of judgment winnows all *evil* with
his eyes.
— Prov. 20:8

"*Evil, evil!*" says the buyer,
but when he goes away he boasts.
— Prov. 20:14

Do not say, "I will repay *evil*,"
wait for the Lord (יהוה Yahweh) and he will help you.
— Prov. 20:22

Blows that wound cleanse away *evil,*
and strokes, the chambers of the heart.
—   Prov. 20:30

The soul of the wicked desires *evil,*
his neighbor finds no grace in his eyes.
—   Prov. 21:10

The righteous one wisely considers (or acts toward) the house of
the wicked,
He is overturning the wicked for *evil.*
—   Prov. 21:12

A shrewd one sees I and hides himself,
but the simple go on and suffer for it.
—   Prov. 22:3, 27:12

Do not eat the bread of (one with) an *evil* eye; do not desire his
delicacies;
for he is like one who is inwardly reckoning,
"Eat and drink!" he says to you, but his heart is not with you.
The bit you have eaten you will vomit, and spoil your pleasant
words.
—   Prov. 23:6-8

Be not envious of *evil* men (אִישׁ ish), nor desire to be with them;
for their minds devise violence and their lips talk of mischief.
—   Prov. 24:1-2

He who devises to do *evil,*
to him, (he) shall be called a lord of *evil* plots.
—   Prov. 24:8

Lie not in ambush as a wicked one at the abode of the righteous,
do not violate his home;
for a righteous one falls seven times, and rises again;
but the wicked shall stumble into *evil.*

When your enemy falls do not rejoice,
and when he stumbles do not let your heart be glad;
lest the Lord see and it be *evil* in his eyes,
and turn away his anger from him.
Fret not yourself because of evildoers,
and be not envious of the wicked;
for there shall be no hereafter for the *evil*;
the lamp of the wicked will be put out.
—   Prov. 24:15-20

(From King Hezekiah's scribes)
Like one who takes off a garment on a cold day and like vinegar on
a wound is one singing with songs on an *evil* heart.
—   Prov. 25:20

As silver overlaid with an earthen vessel,
so are burning lips and a heart of *evil*.
—   Prov. 26:23

The sensible one sees *evil* and hides himself,
—   Prov. 27:12a

Evil men (אִישׁ ish) do not understand justice,
but those who seek the Lord understand it completely.
—   Prov. 28:5

The one leading the upright into an *evil* way will fall into his own
pit;
but the blameless will have a goodly inheritance.
—   Prov. 28:10

And whoso harden his heart falls into *evil*.
—   Prov. 28:14b

A man (אִישׁ ish) with an *evil* eye hastens after wealth,
and does not know that want will come upon him.
—   Prov. 28:22

166

By sin an *evil* man (אִישׁ ish) is ensnared,
—   Prov. 29:6a

(From King Lemuel of Massa)
She hath done him good, and not *evil*,
all days of her life.
—   Prov. 31:12 *(referring to the good wife)*

    <u>evil, trouble, sorrow, wickedness</u> אָוֶן (`aven) (modern: wickedness, evil)

This Hebrew word אָוֶן (`ayen) is similar to the other Hebrew word for evil (רַע rah). One clue to the distinction might be found in Prov. 6:16-19, which speaks of feet that run toward evil and a heart that devises evil אָוֶן. Perhaps, as the one of the definitions, sorrow, suggests, this word אָוֶן is more internal in nature.

A worthless person (אָדָם adam), a man (אִישׁ ish) of *trouble*,
goes about with crooked speech, winks with his eyes, scrapes with
his feet, points with his finger, with perverted heart devises evil,
continually sowing discord,
therefore calamity will come upon him suddenly; in a moment he
will be broken beyond healing.
—   Prov. 6:12-15

There are six things which the Lord (יהוה Yahweh) hates,
seven which are an abomination to him:
haughty eyes, a lying tongue,
and hands that shed innocent blood,
a heart that devises plans of *trouble*,
feet that make haste to run to evil,
a false witness who breathes out lies,
and a man who sows discord among brothers.
—   Prov. 6:16-19

The way of the Lord (יהוה Yahweh) is strength to the perfect,
and ruin to workers of *trouble*.
—   Prov. 10:29

All *trouble* shall not happen to the righteous,
—   Prov. 12:21a

An evil-doer listens to lips of *trouble*,
and a liar gives heed to a tongue of (evil) desire.
—   Prov. 17:4

and the mouth of the wicked devours *trouble*.
—   Prov. 19:28b

When justice is done, it is a joy to the righteous
but dismay to the workers of *trouble*.
—   Prov. 21:15

He who sows injustice will reap *trouble*,
—   Prov. 22:8a

(From Agur of Massa)
So — the way of an adulterous woman,
she hath eaten and hath wiped her mouth,
and hath said, 'I have not done *trouble*.'
—   Prov. 30:20

FOOLS

There are several Hebrew words translated in English loosely as
"fool".

folly, foolishness אִוֶּלֶת (`ivveleth) (modern: foolishness)

Almost all of the uses of this word in the Hebrew Bible are found in Proverbs. One other verse is "O God, Thou — Thou has known concerning my folly, and my desolations from Thee have not been hid," Psalm 69:6

and in the greatness of his (a man's) (אִישׁ ish) *folly* he goes astray.
— Prov. 5:23

but a heart of dullards calls out *folly*.
— Prov. 12:23b

but a dullard flaunts *folly*.
— Prov. 13:16b

but *folly* with her own hands tears it (the house) down.
— Prov. 14:1b

but the *folly* of fools is deceit.
— Prov. 14:8b

He who is short to anger acts *foolishly*,
and the plots of a man is hated.
— Prov. 14:17a

The simple acquire *folly*,
— Prov. 14:18a

the folly of dullards is their *folly*.
— Prov. 14:24b

but one of short spirit exalts *folly*.
— Prov. 14:29b

but a mouth of dullards pours out *folly*.
— Prov. 15:2b

but the mouth of dullards feed on *folly.*
— Prov. 15:14b

Folly is joy to him who lacks heart,
— Prov. 15:21a

but the discipline of fools is *folly.*
— Prov. 16:22b

Let a man (אִישׁ ish) meet a bear robbed of cubs than a dullard in his *folly.*
— Prov. 17:12

If one gives an answer before he hears,
it is his *folly* and shame.
— Prov. 18:13

The *folly* of person (אָדָם adam) brings his way to ruin,
and his heart rages against the Lord.
— Prov. 19:3

Folly is bound up in the heart of a lad,
but the rod of discipline drives it far from him.
— Prov. 22:15

The plotting of *folly* is sin,
— Prov. 24:9a

(From King Hezekiah's scribes)
Answer not a fool according to his *folly,*
lest thou be like to him — even you.
Answer a fool according to his *folly,*
lest he be wise in his own eyes.
— Prov. 26:4-5

As a dog hath returned to its vomit,
a fool is repeating his *folly*.
—   Prov. 26:11

Though you pound a stupid one in a mortar with a pestle along with grain,
yet his *folly* will not depart from him.
—   Prov. 27:22

foolish, stupid   אֱוִיל   (evil) (modern: fool, stupid)

The prophet Isaiah said the princes of Zoan were foolish and the counselors of Pharoah have stupid counsel, 19:11.

He going after her (a whore) is like
an ox going to the slaughter
or as a *stupid* one to the discipline of the stocks.
—   Prov. 7:22

The wise of heart accepts commands,
but the *stupid* of lips shall be thrust away.
—   Prov. 10:8

One winking the eye gives pain,
but the *stupid* of lips shall be thrust away.
—   Prov. 10:10

the mouth of a *stupid* one is near ruin.
—   Prov. 10:14b

but *stupid* ones who lack of heart die.
—   Prov. 10:21b

but a *stupid* one is servant to the wise.
—   Prov. 11:29b

The way of a *stupid* one is right in his own eyes.
— Prov. 12:15a

A *stupid* one's vexation is known in a day,
— Prov. 12:16a

In the mouth of a *stupid* one is a rod of pride,
— Prov. 14:3a

Stupid ones mock at guilt,
— Prov. 14:9

A *stupid* one despises his father's discipline,
— Prov. 15:5a

but the discipline of *stupid* ones is folly.
— Prov. 16:22b

Even a *stupid* one keeping silence is reckoned wise,
he who is shutting his lips intelligent!
— Prov. 17:28

but every *stupid* one reveals himself.
— Prov. 20:3

Too high for a *stupid* one is wisdom,
— Prov. 24:7

(From King Hezekiah's scribes)
A stone is heavy, and sand is weighty,
but a *stupid* one's provocation is heavier than both.
— Prov. 27:3

Crush a *stupid* one in a mortar with a pestle along with crushed
grain,
yet his folly will not depart from him.
— Prov. 27:22

If a wise man (אִישׁ ish) disputes with a *stupid* man (אִישׁ ish), he even shakes or laughs and there is no rest.
— Prov. 29:9

fool, dullard כְּסִיל (kesil) (modern: fool)

The psalmist said that dullards or fools can not understand the works of the Lord, 92:6.

Until when, simple ones, will ... *dullards* hate knowledge?
— Prov. 1:22

and the ease of *dullards* destroys them.
— Prov. 1:32

but the *foolish* exalt ignominy.
— Prov. 3:35

Understand, ye simple ones, prudence,
and, *dullards*, understand heart!
— Prov. 8:5

A woman of *dullness* makes noise
(is) simple and knows nothing.
— Prov. 9:13

but a *dullard* son is the sorrow of his mother.
— Prov. 10:1b

and he who slanders is a *dullard.*
— Prov. 10:18b

As laughter is to the *dullard* in working out evil plots,
so wisdom is to the man (אִישׁ ish) of understanding.
— Prov. 10:23

but the heart of *dullards* calls out folly.
— Prov. 12:23b

but a *dullard* flaunts his folly.
— Prov. 13:16b

but it is hateful to *dullards* to depart from evil.
— Prov. 13:19b

but a companion of *dullards* suffers evil.
— Prov. 13:20b

but the folly of *dullards* is deceit.
— Prov. 14:8b

A wise one fears and departs from evil,
but the *dullard* passes over and is bold.
— Prov. 14:16

but the folly of *dullards* is folly.
— Prov. 14:24b

but a mouth of *dullards* pours out folly.
— Prov. 15:2b

The lips of the wise scatter knowledge,
but the heart of *dullards* is not so.
— Prov. 15:7

but mouths of *dullards* feed on folly.
— Prov. 15:14b

but a *dull person* (אָדָם adam) despises his mother.
— Prov. 15:20b

A rebuke goes into a discerning one more than 100 blows into a *dullard.*
—   Prov. 17:10

Let a man (אִישׁ ish) meet a bear robbed of cubs than a *dullard* in his folly.
—   Prov. 17:12

Why is there a price in the hand of a *dullard* to buy wisdom, and not a mind?
—   Prov. 17:16

He who fathers a *dullard* falls into grief for it,
and the father of a senseless one will not rejoice over it.
—   Prov. 17:21b

but the eyes of a *dullard* are on the ends of the earth.
—   Prov. 17:24

An indignation to his father is a *dull* son,
and bitterness to her who bore him.
—   Prov. 17:25

A *dullard* takes no pleasure in understanding,
but only in expressing his opinion.
—   Prov. 18:2

A *dullard*'s lips bring strife,
and his mouth invites a flogging.
A *dullard's* mouth is his ruin,
and his lips are a snare to himself.
—   Prov. 18:6-7

Better is a poor man who walks in his integrity
than one who is crooked in speech and he (who) is a *dullard.*
—   Prov. 19:1

Luxury is not fitting for a *dullard,*
— Prov. 19:10

and blows (are prepared) for the backs of *dullards.*
— Prov. 19:29

A desirable treasure and oil are in a wise man's dwelling,
but a *dull* person (אָדָם adam) devours it.
— Prov. 21:20

Do not speak in the hearing of a *dullard,*
for he will despise the wisdom of your words.
— Prov. 23:9

(From King Hezekiah's scribes)
Like snow in summer or rain in harvest,
so honor is not fitting for a fool.
Like a sparrow in its flitting, like a swallow in its flying,
a curse that is causeless does not alight.
A whip for the horse, a bridle for the ass,
and a rod for the back of *dullards.*
Answer not a *dullard* according to his folly,
lest he be wise in his own eyes.
He who sends a message by the hand of a *dullard*
cuts off his own feet and drinks violence.
Like the legs of a lame, which hang useless,
is a proverb in the mouth of *dullards.*
Like one who binds the stone in the sling
is he who gives honor to a *dullard.*
Like a thorn that goes up into the hand of a drunkard
is a proverb in the mouth of *dullards.*
Like an archer who wounds everybody
is he who hires a passing *dullard* or drunkard.
Like a dog that returns to his own vomit
is a fool that repeats his folly.

Do you see a man (אִישׁ ish) wise in his own eyes?
There is more hope for a *dullard* than for him.
— Prov. 26:1-12

One who trusts in his own mind is a *dullard*,
— Prov. 28:26a

A *dullard* brings out all of his spirit
but the wise holding it back quiets it.
— Prov. 29:11

Do you see a man (אִישׁ ish) hasty in his words?
There is more hope for a *dullard* than for him.
— Prov. 29:20

foolish, ignoble,senseless נָבָל (naval) (modern: villain, rascal,
scoundrel)

In II Sam. 3:33, King David lamented whether his trusted aide
Abner had died senselessly.)

Lips of excess (RSV: Fine speech) is not fitting a *senseless* one,
much less lying lips for a prince.
— Prov. 17:7

He who fathers a dullard falls into grief for it,
and the father of a *senseless* one will not rejoice over it.
— Prov. 17:21b

(From Agur of Massa)
Under three things the earth quakes;
under four it cannot bear up:
when a servant reigns, and when a *senseless* one is filled with
food;
and a hated (woman) is married,
and a handmaid when she succeeds her mistress.
— Prov. 30:21-23

If you have been *senseless*, exalting yourself,
or if you have plotting, put your hand on your mouth.
— Prov. 30:32

Hate
See love and hate, "Chapter 1: Our Emotions"

Perverse
(The primary meaning of the following words is "perverse.")

bent, twisted לוז (luz) (modern: hazel, almond, a meaning that
was used in Gen. 30:37)

*The Holy One of Israel said that because the people's trust was
bent and twisted, iniquity would come down crashing on them,
Isaiah 30:12-13..*

Whose paths are crooked and *bent* in their tracks,
— Prov. 2:15

My son! let them not *turn* from your eyes,
 Keep wisdom and thoughtfulness,
— Prov. 3:21

For hateful to the Lord (יהוה Yahweh) is the *bent* (i.e. perverse),
— Prov. 3:32

Turn away from the crooked mouth and *twisted* lips.
— Prov. 4:24

but one *bent* in his way despises Him (the Lord).
— Prov. 14:2b

crooked עִקֵּשׁ ('iqqesh) (modern: stubborn, perverted)

*Moses told the assembly of Israelites in Deut. 32:5 they were a
stubborn generation.)*

Turn away from the *crooked* of mouth
and put far from you deviious lips.
—   Prov. 4:24

A worthless evil man walks with a *crooked* mouth.
—   Prov. 6:12

in my words is not a twisted and *crooked* thing.
—   Prov. 8:8

One who makes *crooked* his ways shall be knows.
—   Prov. 10:9b

An abomination to the Lord (יהוה Yahweh) is a *crooked* heart,
—   Prov. 11:20

One of *crooked* heart does not find good,
and perverse in his tongue falls into evil.
—   Pro. 17:20

A poor one who walks in integrity
is better than one *crooked* in his lips and he is a fool.
—   Prov. 19:1

Thorns and snares are in the way of the *crooked,*
he who guards himself will keep far from them.
—   Prov. 22:5

(From King Hezekiah's scribes)
Better is a poor one who walks in his integrity
than the two ways of the *crooked* even if he is rich.
—   Prov. 28:6

One who walks in integrity will be delivered,
but he who is *crooked* in his ways will fall into a pit.
—   Prov. 28:18

179

fickle, froward תַהְפּוּכָה (tahpukhah) (modern: fickle, wayward)

The Lord said he would hide his face from the Israelites because they were a froward generation "in whom there is no faithfulness," Deut. 32:20. Notice how frequently the word is used in connction with the mouth or what is spoken.

To deliver you from the way of evil,
and from the men (אִישׁ ish) speaking *froward* things....
they delight in *frowardness* of the wicked,
—   Prov. 2:12, 14b

the way of evil and the *froward* mouth I hate.
—   Prov. 8:13b

the mouth of the wicked is *froward*...
and the mouth of the wicked *froward!*
—   Prov. 10:31b, 32b

A man (אִישׁ ish) who is *froward* sends out contentiousness,
—   Prov. 16:28

One who shuts his eyes to plan *froward* things pressing his lips brings to pass evil.
—   Prov. 16:30

Fickle is the way of a guilty man (אִישׁ ish),
but the work of the pure is upright.
—   Prov. 21:8

Your eyes shall look on strange women,
and your heart will speak *froward* things.
—   Prov. 23:33

perverted, twisted, crooked סָלַף (selef) (modern: distort, falsify)

The Lord said that the people were not to take bribes because these pervert the cause of the righteous, Ex. 23:8 and Deut. 16:19. The word is very similar to the Hebrew word for overthrow.

but the *pervertness* of traitors destroys them.
— Prov. 11:3

but *pervertedness* (in a tongue) is a breaking in the spirit.
— Prov. 15:4

The folly of a person (אָדָם adam) makes *perverted* his way and against the Lord (יְהוָה ish) his heart rages.
— Prov. 19:3

also:

perverse נָעֲוֶה (na'aveh) (modern: distorted, crooked)

This word appears only once in the Hebrew Bible.

but the *perverse* of heart shall become despised.
— Prov. 12:8

Pride

comely, adorning, beautifying גֵּאָה (ge'ah) (modern: becoming, fine, good-looking)

This Hebrew word seems quite benign; yet, the Hebrew Bible seems to rail against it, perhaps its use in the excess. The psalmist seeks to "render to the proud their deserts!" 94:2 and protests that "the proud hid a snare for me," 140:5.

The fear of the Lord (יהוה Yahweh) is to hate ... *adorning* and loftiness,
— Prov. 8:13a

In the mouth of a stupid one is a rod of *adorning.*
— Prov. 14:3

The house of the *adorning* the Lord (יהוה Yahweh) pulls down,
— Prov. 15:25a

Before destruction goes *adorning* and a haughty spirit before stumbling.
Better is lowness of spirit with the afflicted than to divide the spoil with the adorned.
— Prov. 16:18-19

(From King Hezekiah's scribes)
A person's (אָדָם adam) *adorning* brings him low,
but the humble of spirit takes hold of honor.
— Prov. 29:23

    <u>arrogant</u> יָהִיר (yahir) (modern: arrogant, boastful, proud)

This word appears only once in the Hebrew Bible.

Insolent, *arrogant* – scoffer is his name who deals in the wrath of insolence.
— Prov. 21:24

    <u>insolent, presumptuous</u> זָדוֹן (zadon) (modern: malice, wickedness)

Habakkuk 2:5 suggests that wine makes a virile man (גֶּבֶר gever) insolent.

Comes *insolence*, then comes shame.
— Prov. 11:2

Only by *insolence* comes strife,
—   Prov. 13:10

Insolent, arrogant – scoffer is his name who deals in the wrath of *insolence*.
—   Prov. 21:24

proud, haughty רָחָב (rakhav) (modern: arrogant, boasting)

Almost always in other biblical uses, the word means wide or broad, perhaps suggesting that in the following, pride had grown into haughtiness.

Lifted eyes and a *haughty* heart,
the lamp of the wicked, are sin.
—   Prov. 21:4

vain הֶבֶל (hevel) (modern: vain, futile)

The Israelites had provoked the Lord God with their vanities, I Kings 16:13, 26

Wealth from *vanity* becomes little,
—   Prov. 13:11

The making of treasures by a lying tongue,
a *vanity* driven away of those seeking death.
—   Prov. 21:6

(From King Lemuel of Massa)
beauty is *vain*
—   Prov. 31:30b

haughty גָּבֹהַּ (gavoah) (modern: vain, futile)

This word also has a meaning of height, suggesting that pride can grow to the level of haughtiness. Hannah's prayer said not to talk very haughtily, I Samuel 2:3.

An abomination to the lord is everyone *haughty* in heart,
—   Prov. 16:5

Before destruction goes adorning and a *haughty* spirit before stumbling.
—   Prov. 16:18

Whoso is making *haughty* his entrance is seeking destruction.
—   Prov. 17:19

Before destruction a man's heart (אִישׁ ish) is *haughty*,
—   Prov. 18:12

also

(From King Hezekiah's scribes)
It is not good to eat much honey,
and to search out glory as glory.
—   Prov. 25:27

Reproach

to dig, to be put to shame חָפַר (hafar) (modern: dig, digger)

Psalms 7:15 suggests the old saw, "you dig your own hole," a s example of shame or reproach.

And the wicked causes abhorrence, and is *reproached*,
—   Prov. 13:5b

The son who assaults his father and chases away his mother causes shame and brings *reproach.*
— Prov. 19:26

reproach, taunt, defy חֶרְפָּה (herpah) (modern: disgrace, shame)

When Rachel conceived, she said God had taken away her reproach, according to Gen. 30:23. God told Joshua that he had rolled the reproach of Egypt off the Israelites, Josh. 5:9.)

and his (one committing adultery) *reproach* shall not be wiped away.
— Prov. 6:33

The one oppressing the poor *reproaches* his maker,
— Prov. 14:31

When wickedness comes ... comes also *reproach*
— Prov. 18:3a

(From King Hezekiah's scribes)
Be wise, my son,
 and give joy to my heart
so that I may return my *reproacher* a word.
— Prov. 27:11

Scoffer, scorner לֵיץ (lets) (modern: joker, jester)

According to II Chron. 30, the Israelites scoffed at Hezekiah's couriers relaying the king's directive to take part in the passover in Jerusalem.

Until when, simple ones, will you love simplicity,
and *scoffers* will desire scoffing for them?
— Prov. 1:22

If he scoffs at the *scoffers*,
yet to the lowly he gives grace.
—   Prov. 3:34

One rebuking a *scoffer* takes shame for himself ...
Do not reprove a *scoffer* lest he hate you.
—   Prov. 9:7a, 8a

and if you *scoff* you alone will bear it.
—   Prov. 9:12

but a *scoffer* does not listen to rebuke.
—   Prov. 13:1

A *scoffer* seeks wisdom in vain,
—   Prov. 14:6b

A *scoffer* does not love one who corrects him,
he will not go to the wise.
—   Prov. 15:12

Strike a *scoffer*, and the simple will be shrewd,
—   Prov. 19:25a

A worthless witness *scoffs* at justice,
—   Prov. 19:28a

Judgments are prepared for *scoffers*,
—   Prov. 19:29

Wine is a *scoffer*, strong drink a brawler,
—   Prov. 20:1a

When the *scoffer* is punished, the simple becomes wise,
—   Prov. 21:11a

Proud and arrogant – *scoffer* is his name who deals in the wrath of pride.
—Prov. 21:24

Drive out a *scoffer*, and strife will go out,
and quarrels and shame will cease.
— Prov. 22:10

and the *scoffer* is an abomination to persons (אָדָם adam).
— Prov. 24:9b

(From King Hezekiah's scribes)
Men (אִישׁ ish) of *scorn* set a city aflame,
— Prov. 29:8a

Shame

shame, bashfulness, shy בּוּשׁ (bosh) (modern: diffident, shy, coy)

When Adam and Eve realized they were naked, they were ashamd, Gen. 2:25

one who sleeps in harvest is a son causing *shame*.
— Prov. 10:5

but (the king's) wrath is upon the one causing *shame*.
— Prov. 14:35

A servant who acts prudently will rule over a son who acts *shamefully*,
and will share the inheritance as one of the brothers.
— Prov. 17:2

The son who assaults his father and chases away his mother causes *shame* and brings reproach.
— Prov. 19:26

(From King Hezekiah's scribes)
but a youth sent away causes his mother *shame*.
—   Prov. 29:15

    shame, ignominy, disgrace, dishonor קָלוֹן (qalon) (modern:
dishonor, shame)

According to their abundance so they sinned against Me, Their
honour into shame I change, Hosea 4:7

but the dullard exalts *disgrace*.
—   Prov. 3:35

A stroke and shame he (a thief) does find,
and his *ignominy* is not wiped away,
—   Prov. 6:33

One rebuking a scoffer takes for himself *ignominy*.
—   Prov. 9:7a

Comes insolence, then comes *ignominy*.
—   Prov. 11:2

but the astute cover *ignominy*.
—   Prov. 12:16

Poverty and *ignominy* for one ignoring chastisement,
—   Prov. 13:18a

and with *ignominy* comes reproach.
—   Prov. 18:3b

Drive out the scoffer,
and contentiousness will go out,
lawsuits and *ignominy* will cease.
—   Prov. 22:10

shame, insult, reproach, humiliation כְּלִמָּה (kelimmah)
(modern: causing shame)

The makers of idols are put to humiliation and confusion, Isaiah 45:16.

If one gives an answer before he hears,
it is folly and to him *humiliation.*
—   Prov. 18:13

also:

(From King Hezekiah's scribes)

Do not go out to fight hastily,
lest what you shall do, in the end of it, make you blush.
Plead your cause with your neighbor
and do not reveal the secret of another,
lest the one who hears you put you to shame
and your evil report turns not away.
—   Prov. 25:8-10

Simple-minded, fool פְּתִי (pethi) (modern: simpleton, fool)

The Lord preserves the simple, Psalms 116:6, and the testimony of the Lord makes wise the simple, Psalms 19:7.

Until when, *simple* ones, will you love *simplicity?*
—   Prov. 1:22

For the going astray of the *simple* kills them,
—   Prov. 1:32

I saw among the *simple* ones,
I observed among the sons youth lacking of heart.
—   Prov. 7:7

Understand, *simple* ones, astuteness.
—   Prov. 8:5

Who is *simple*, turn aside here!,
—   Prov. 9:4a, 16a

Forsake ye, the *simple*, and live,
and be happy in the way of understanding.
—   Prov. 9:6

A dull woman ... is *simple* and knows not what.
—   Prov. 9:13

The *simple* believes every word,
—   Prov. 14:15a

The *simple* inherit folly,
—   Prov. 14:18a

Strike a scoffer, and the *simple* will be shrewd,
—   Prov. 19:25a

When the scoffer is punished, the *simple* becomes wise,
—   Prov. 21:11a

A shrewd one sees evil and hides himself,
but the *simple* go on and suffer for it.
—   Prov. 22:3, 27:12

Sin

sin, guilt   חַטָּאת (hatta'th) (modern: sin, fault)

David used this word in Psalms 51:5 as well as I Chron. 21:8 to refer to his affair with Bathsheba. In fact, he used two or three Hebrew words for sin and iniquity, perhaps suggesting how deeply he felt his guilt.

My son, if *guilty* entice you, do not consent.
If they say, "Come with us, let us lie in wait for blood,
let us wantonly ambush the innocent;
like Sheol let us swallow them alive and whole,
like those who go down to the Pit;
we shall find all precious goods,
we shall fill our houses with spoil;
throw in your lot with us,
we will all have one purse" –
My son do not walk in the way of them,
hold back your foot from their paths;
for their feet run to evil,
and they make haste to shed blood.
For in vain is a net spread in the sight of any bird;
for these men lie in wait for their own blood,
they set an ambush for their own lives.
Such are the ways of all who get gain by violence;
it takes away the life of its possessors.
—   Prov. 1:10-19

The wrongs of the wicked ensnare him,
and he is caught in the toils of his *guilt.*
—   Prov. 5:22

the gain of the wicked is for *sin.*
—   Prov. 10:16b

The *guilty* are pursued by evil,
—   Prov. 13:21a

but the *guilty*'s wealth is laid up for the righteous.
—   Prov. 13:22a

He who despises his neighbor is *guilty,*
—   Prov. 14:21a

Righteousness exalts a nation,
but shame to a people is *guilt*.
—   Prov. 14:34

The dread of a king is like the roar of a lion,
he who provokes him to anger is *guilty* against his own soul
(forfeits his life).
—   Prov. 20:2

Who can say, "I have made my heart pure,
I am cleansed from my *guilt*"?
—   Prov. 20:9

Lifted eyes and a haughty heart,
the lamp of the wicked, are *guilty*.
—   Prov. 21:4

The plotting of folly is *guilt*.
—   Prov. 24:9

   sin, perversion, wrong עָוֹן ('an) (modern: sin, crime, offense)

*The Lord God said he would visit the perversities of the father on
the third and fourth generations, Ex. 20:5. Here again David also
used this word in Psalms 51 and I Chron. 21:8 to refer to his affair
with Bathsheba.*

The wrongs of the wicked ensnare him,
and he is caught in the toils of his *perversity*.
—   Prov. 5:22

In mercy and truth is pardoned *perversity*.
—   Prov. 16:6a

<u>sin, transgression</u> פֶּשַׁע (pesha') (modern: crime, sin, felony)

Jacob asked Laban what crime he had committed, Gen. 31:36. David also used this word in Psalm 51:1 to refer to his affair with Bathsheba. Note the modern Hebrew deepens the biblical use to a felony, and observe how neatly this fits the example of Jacob and Laban as well as Prov. 28:24.

In abundance of words *felonies* cease not,
—   Prov. 10:19

In the *felony* of the lips is the snare of evil,
—   Prov. 12:13

He who covers a *felony* seeks love,
—   Prov. 17:9a

He who loves *felony* exalts strife,
he who makes his door high seeks destruction.
—   Prov. 17:19

and it is (a person's) (אָדָם adam) glory to pass over a *crime*.
—   Prov. 19:11b

(From Kng Hezekiah's scribes)
By *crime* in a land, it has many rulers,
—   Prov. 28:2

One who hides his *felonies* will not fare well
but one confession and leaving them has pity.
—   Prov. 28:13

for a piece of bread a virile man (גֶּבֶר gbr) will commit a *felony*.
—   Prov. 28:21

One who robs his father or his mother and says,
"It is not a *crime*,"
he is a partner to a man (אִישׁ ish) who destroys.
— Prov. 28:24

By *crime*, evil snares a man (אִישׁ ish)
— Prov. 29:6a

When the wicked multiply, *felony* increases;
but the righteous shall see their fall.
— Prov. 29:16

a lord of burning anger abounds in *crime*.
— Prov. 29:22

   guilt אָשָׁם (ashm) (modern: guilt)

Abimelech told Isaac that he could have brought guilt on him by saying Rebecca was his sister, Gen. 26:10.

Fools mock at *guilt,*
— Prov. 14:9a

   Traitors, treacherous בֶּגֶד (beged) (modern: betray)

The Bible uses this word in describing Rebecca's putting Esau's cloak on Jacob to deceive Isaac, Gen. 27:15.

and the *traitors* shall be uprooted from it (the earth).
— Prov. 2:22

but the crookedness of the *traitors* destroys them.
— Prov. 11:3b

but the *traitors* are taken captive by their own lust.
— Prov. 11:6b

but the soul of the *traitor* eats violence.
—   Prov. 13:2

Good insight gives grace,
but the way of *traitors* is continual.
—   Prov. 13:15

A ransom for the righteous shall be the wicked,
and in place of the upright, the *traitors.*
—   Prov. 21:18

and He (the Lord) overthrows the words of the *traitors.*
—   Prov. 22:12

and she (a whore) increases *traitors* among persons (אָדָם adam).
—   Prov. 23:28

Vanity

      emptiness, vanity, nothingness רֵיק (req) (modern: empty,
vacant, blank)

Genesis uses this word in describing the "empty" pit into which
his brothers tossed Joseph at Dothan, 37:1, and Judges 7 similarly
says Gideon's jars were "empty."

(From King Hezekiah's scribes)
He who tills his land will have plenty of bread,
but he who follows *vanities* will have plenty of poverty.
—   Prov. 28:19

      vanity, nothingness, worthlessness שָׁוְא (shav`) (modern:
lie,untruth, vanity)

The Lord admonishes us not to take His name in vain, Exodus 20:7
and Deuteronomy 3:11)

(From Agur of Massa)
Two things I ask of thee;
deny them not to me before I die:
Vanity and the word of a lie remove far from me
poverty and riches do not give to me,
lest I be full and deny thee
and say, "Who is the Lord (יהוה Yahweh)?"
or lest I be poor, and steal,
and profane the name of my God (אֱלֹהִים Elohim).
—   Prov. 30:7-9

vapor, hot air, vanity הֶבֶל (hevel) (modern: vapor, nonsense)

During several unsuccessful kings of Israel, the Lord God was angered by the Israelites' hot air, or vanities, I Kings 16:13, 26, and in the last days of the kingdom, Israel went "after vanity and became vanity," or, "became hot air," II Kings 17:15.)

Wealth from *hot air* will dwindle,
—   Prov. 13:11

The getting of treasures by a lying tongue is *hot air*,
—   Prov. 21:6

Vengeance נָקָם (naqam) (modern: avenge, revenge)

The Lord warned that if anyone killed Cain, it would be avenged seven times, Gen. 4:15).

For jealousy is the burning anger of a virile man (גֶּבֶר gbr)
and he will not spare in the day of *vengeance*.
—   Prov. 6:34

also:

Do not say, "I will repay evil,"
wait for the Lord (יהוה Yahweh) and he will help you.

— Prov. 20:22

Do not say, as he has done to me I will do to him,
I will repay each man (אִישׁ ish) according to his work.
— Prov. 24:29

Wicked, viciousness, offense רָשָׁע (rasha') (modern: wicked, evil,
villain)

*Abraham asked the Lord whether he would destroy the righteous
with the wicked, Gen. 18:23*

But the *wicked* will be cut off from the land,
and the treacherous will be rooted out of it.
— Prov. 2:22

Do not be afraid from sudden dread,
and of the ruin of the *wicked*,
for it is coming.
— Prov. 3:25

The Lord (יהוה Yahweh)'s curse is on the house of the *wicked*,
but he blesses the abode of the righteous.
— Prov. 3:33

Do not enter the path of the *wicked*,
and do not walk in the way of evil ones.
Avoid it; do not go on it and pass on.
For they cannot sleep unless they have done wrong;
they are robbed of sleep unless they have made some one stumble.
For they eat the bread of *wickedness* and drink the wine of
violence.
But the path of the righteous is like the light of dawn,
which shines brighter and brighter until full day.
The way of the *wicked* is like deep darkness;
they do not know over what they stumble.
— Prov. 4:14-19

The iniquities of the *wicked* ensnare him,
and he is caught in the toils of his sin.
— Prov. 5:22

and an abomination to my lips is *wickedness*.
— Prov. 8:7

and he who reproves a *wicked* one incurs injury.
— Prov. 9:7

Treasures gained by *wickedness* do not profit,
— Prov. 10:2a

but the desire of the *wicked* he (the Lord) pushes away.
— Prov. 10:3b

but the mouth of the *wicked* conceals violence.
— Prov. 10:6b, 11b

but the name of the *wicked* will rot.
— Prov. 10:7b

the gain of the *wicked* is sin.
— Prov 10:16b

the heart of the *wicked* is of little worth.
— Prov. 10:20b

What the *wicked* dreads will come upon him,
but the desire of the righteous will be granted.
When the tempest passes, the *wicked* is no more,
but the righteous is established for ever.
— Prov. 10:24-25

but the years of the *wicked* will be shortened.
The hope of the righteous is joy,
but the expectation of the *wicked* shall perish.

The Lord (יהוה Yahweh) is a stronghold to him whose way is upright,
but destruction to evildoers.
The righteous will never be removed,
but the *wicked* will not dwell in the land.
The mouth of the righteous brings forth wisdom,
but the perverse tongue will be cutoff.
The lips of the righteous know what is acceptable,
but the mouth of the *wicked*, what is perverse.
— Prov. 10:27b-32

but righteousness delivers from death.
The righteousness of the blameless keeps his way straight,
by his *wickedness* the *wicked* fail.
The righteousness of the upright delivers them,
but the treacherous are taken captive by their lust.
In the death of a *wicked* person (אדם adam), his hope perishes,
and the expectation of the godless comes to nought.
The righteous is delivered from trouble,
and the *wicked* gets into it instead.
With his mouth the godless one would destroy his neighbor,
but by knowledge the righteous are delivered.
When the righteous prosper, the city rejoices,
and when the *wicked* perish there is singing.
By the blessing of the upright a city is exalted,
but is overthrown by the mouth of the *wicked*.
— Prov. 11:4b-11

A *wicked* one earns deceptive wages,
— Prov. 11:18a

the hope of the *wicked* (ends) in wrath.
— Prov. 11:23b

If the righteous is repaid on earth,
how much more the *wicked* and the sinner!
— Prov. 11:31

but a man (אִישׁ ish) of evil plots is *wicked*.
— Prov. 12:2

A person (אָדָם adam) is not established by wickedness,
— Prov. 12:3a

The counsels of the *wicked* are deceit.
The words of the *wicked* lie in wait for blood,
— Prov. 12:5b-6a

The *wicked* are overthrown and are no more,
— Prov. 12:7a

but the pity of the *wicked* is cruel.
— Prov. 12:10a

The *wicked* desire the net of evils,
— Prov. 12:12a

but the *wicked* will be filled with evil.
— Prov. 12:21b

but the way of the *wicked* leads them astray.
— Prov. 12:26b

but the *wicked* acts shamefully and disgracefully ...
but sin overthrows the *wicked*.
— Prov. 13:5b, 6b

but the lamp of the *wicked* will be put out.
— Prov. 13:9b

A *wicked* messenger plunges into evil,
but a faithful ambassador is healing.
— Prov. 13:17

but the belly of the *wicked* suffers.
—   Prov. 13:25

The house of the *wicked* will be destroyed,
—   Prov. 14:11a

the *wicked* (bow down) at the gates of the righteous.
—   Prov. 14:19b

In his evil-doing the *wicked* is overthrown,
—   Prov. 14:32a

but the increase of the *wicked* is trouble.
—   Prov. 15:6b

The sacrifice of the *wicked* is an abomination to the Lord (יהוה
Yahweh) ....
An abomination to the Lord (יהוה Yahweh) is the way of the
wicked.
—   Prov. 15:8a, 9a

but the mouth of the *wicked* pours out evil things.
—   Prov. 15:28

The Lord (יהוה Yahweh) is far from the *wicked,*
—   Prov. 15:29a

The Lord (יהוה Yahweh) has made everything for its purpose,
even the *wicked* for the day of trouble.
—   Prov. 16:4

It is an abomination for kings to commit *wickedness,*
for by righteousness the throne is set.
—   Prov. 16:12

One who justifies the *wicked* and condemns the righteous
is an abomination to the Lord (יהוה Yahweh), even both of them.
—   Prov. 17:15

The *wicked* takes a bribe from the bosom to stretch the ways of
justice.
—   Prov. 17:23

When *wickedness* comes, comes also scorn with shame.
—   Prov. 18:3a

To lift up the face of the *wicked* is not good,
—   Prov. 18:5a

and the mouth of the *wicked* devours evil.
—   Prov. 19:28b

A wise king winnows the *wicked,*
and drives the wheel over them.
—   Prov. 20:26

Lifted eyes and a proud heart,
the lamp of the *wicked*, are sin.
—   Prov. 21:4

The violence of the *wicked* ensnares them
because they refuse to do justice.
—   Prov. 21:7

The soul of the *wicked* desires evil,
his neighbor finds no grace in his eyes.
—   Prov. 21:10

The righteous one wisely considers the house of the *wicked*,
He overturns the wicked for evil.
—   Prov. 21:12

A ransom for the righteous is the *wicked,*
—   Prov. 21:18a

The sacrifice of the *wicked* is an abomination,
how much more when he brings with it evil intent.
—   Prov. 21:27

A *wicked* man (אִישׁ ish) hardens his face,
—   Prov. 21:29a

Lie not in ambush, O *wicked* one, at the abode of the righteous,
do not violate his home;
for a righteous one falls seven times, and rises again;
but the *wicked* shall stumble into evil.
—   Prov. 24:15-16

Fret not yourself because of evildoers,
and be not envy the *wicked*;
for there shall be no hereafter for the evil;
the lamp of the *wicked* will be put out.
—   Prov. 24:19-20

He who says to the *wicked,* "You are innocent,"
will be cursed by peoples, abhorred by nations;
but those who rebuke (the wicked) will have delight,
and a good blessing will be upon them.
—   Prov. 24:24-25

(From King Hezekiah's scribes)
Take away the *wicked* from the presence of the king,
and his throne shall be established in righteousness.
—   Prov. 25:5

Like a fouled spring or a polluted fountain
is the righteous tottering before the *wicked.*
—   Prov. 25:26

The wicked flee when no one is pursuing,
but the righteous are as bold as a lion.
—   Prov. 28:1

Forsakers of the law praise the wicked,
but keepers of the law strive against them.
—   Prov. 28:4

When the righteous rejoice great is the glory,
but when the *wicked* rise a person (אָדָם adam) will be sought.
—   Prov. 28:12

Like a roaring bear and a charging lion is a *wicked* ruler of a weak
people.
—   Prov. 28:15

When the *wicked* rise, a person (אָדָם adam) hides himself,
but when they perish, the righteous multiply.
—   Prov. 28:28

When the righteous increase, the people rejoice;
but when the *wicked* rule, the people groan.
—   Prov. 29:2

a *wicked* one does not discern knowledge.
—   Prov. 29:7b

A ruler who listens to a lying word,
all his ministers are *wicked*.
—   Prov. 29:12

When the *wicked* multiply, transgression increases,
but the righteous shall see their fall.
—   Prov. 29:16

An abomination to the righteous is an unjust man (אִישׁ ish),
and an abomination to the *wicked* is the way of the upright.
—   Prov. 29:27

Chapter 6: GLUTTONY AND DRINKING

The righteous eats to his soul's satisfaction,
but the belly of the wicked suffers.
—   Prov. 13:25

Better is a dinner of herbs where love is,
than a fatted ox and hatred with it.
—   Prov. 15:17

The lazy one buries his hand in the dish,
and will not even bring it back to his mouth.
—   Prov. 19:24

Wine is a scoffer, strong drink a brawler,
and whoever is led astray by it is not wise.
—   Prov. 20:1

Bread gained by a lie is sweet to a man (אִישׁ ish),
but afterward his mouth will be full of gravel.
—   Prov. 20:17

A man (אִישׁ ish) who loves joy will be poor,
he who loves wine and oil will not be rich.
—   Prov. 21:17

When you sit down to eat with a ruler,
observe carefully what is before you;
and put a knife to your throat if you are a possessor of appetite.
Do not desire his delicacies for it is the bread of lies.
—   Prov. 23:1-3

Be not among winebibbers, or among gluttonous eaters of meat;
for the drunkard and the glutton will come to poverty,
and drowsiness will clothe one with rags.
— Prov. 23:20-21

Who has woe? Who has sorrow? Who has strife? Who has complaining?
Who has wounds without cause? Who has redness of eyes?
Those who tarry long over wine, those who go to try mixed wine,
Do not look at wine when it is red,
when it sparkles in the cup and goes down smoothly.
At the last it bites like a serpent, and stings like an adder.
Your eyes will see strange women
and your heart shall speak perverse things.
You will be like one who lies on the top of a mast.
"They struck me," you will say, "but I was not hurt.
They beat me, but I did not feel it.
When shall I awake? I will seek another drink."
— Prov. 23:29-35

My son, eat honey, for it is good,
and the drippings of the honeycomb are sweet to your taste.
— Prov. 24:13

(From King Hezekiah's scribes)
Like cold water to a thirsty soul,
so is good news from a far country.
— Prov. 25:25

If you have found honey, eat only enough for you,
lest you be sated with it and vomit it.
— Prov. 25:16

It is not good to eat much honey,
and to search out glory as glory.
— Prov. 25:27

As a thorn goes up into the hand of a drunkard,
so a parable in the mouth of dullards.
—   Prov. 26:9

The lazy buries his hand in the dish,
he is weary to bring it back to his mouth.
—   Prov. 26:15

He who is sated loathes honey,
but to one who is hungry everything bitter is sweet.
—   Prov. 27:8

(From Agur of Massa)
So the way of an adulterous woman,
she eats and wipes her mouth,
and says, I have not done any evil.
—   Prov. 30:20

(From King Lemuel of Massa)
It is not for kings, O Lemuel,
it is not for kings to drink wine,
or for rulers to desire strong drink;
lest they drink and forget what has been decreed,
and pervert the rights of all the afflicted.
Give strong drink to him who is perishing,
and wine to those in bitter distress;
let them drink and forget their poverty,
and remember their misery no more.
—   Prov. 31:4-7

PART II: OUR WORLD

Chapter 7: ECONOMIC MATTERS

Economic justice and injustice

See also the poor, afflicted and destitute entries below. There are many other entries of this word in "Justice and Injustice" in Chapter XI: Principles, and Political Justice and Injustice," in Chapter VIII: Political Matters.

to judge, to administer justice שָׁפַט (shafat) (modern: judge, referee)

(From King Lemuel of Massa)
Open thy mouth, *judge* righteously,
both the cause of the poor and needy!'
—   Prov. 31:9

judgment, right מִשְׁפָּט   (mishpat) (modern: judgment)

The poor one's fallow land produces much food,
but it is swept away when there is no *judgment*.
—   Prov. 13:23

oppression עֹשֶׁק ('esheq) (modern: exploit, subdue, rob)

The psalmist says not to set one's heart on oppression, robbery or wealth, 62:10.

He *oppresses* the poor insults his maker,
—   Prov. 14:31a

One who *oppresses* the poor to increase his own wealth,
or gives to the rich, will only come to want.
— Prov. 22:16

(From King Hzekiah's scribes)
A poor man virile (גֶּבֶר gbr) who *oppresses* the poor is a
sweeping rain that leaves no food.
— Prov. 28:3

violence חָמָס (hamas) (modern: corruption, violence)

God told Noah the earth was filled with violence, Genesis 6: 11, 13

For they (the wicked) eat the bread of wickedness and drink the
wine of *violence*.
— Prov. 4:17

but the mouth of the wicked covers *violence*.
— Prov. 10:6b, 11b

also:

Do not rob the poor, because he is poor,
or crush the afflicted at the gate;
for the Lord (יהוה Yahweh) will plead their cause and despoil of
life those who despoil them.
— Prov. 22:22-23

Do not ... enter the fields of the fatherless;
for their Redeemer is strong;
he will plead their cause against you.
— Prov. 23:10-11

slaves, servants עֶבֶד ('eved) (modern: slave, servant)

*The Lord God sent man away from the Garden of Eden to "serve"
– or till – the land, Genesis 3:23.*

and the fool will be *servant* to the wise.
—   Prov. 11:29

Better is one who is despised and has a *servant*
than one who honors himself but lacks bread.
—   Prov. 12:9

One who is tilling — i.e., *"serving"* — the ground is satisfied with
bread,
—   Prov. 12:11

A *servant* who deals wisely has the king's favor,
but his wrath falls on one who acts shamefully.
—   Prov. 14:35

A wise *servant* ruleth over a son causing shame,
 And in the midst of brethren he shares an inheritance..
—   Prov. 17:2

Luxury is not comely for a fool,
much less for a *slave* to rule among princes.
—   Prov. 19:10

The rich rules over the poor,
 and the borrower is the *slave* of the lender.
—-   Prov. 22:7

(From King Hezekiah's scribes)
By words a *servant* is not corrected,
for though he understands, there is no answer.
—   Prov. 29:19

He who pampers his *servant* from youth
will in the end find him as his successor.
—   Prov. 29:21

(From Agur of Massa)
Do not slander a *servant* to his master,
lest he curse you and you be held guilty.
—   Prov. 30:10

Under three things the earth trembles;
under four it cannot bear up;
when a *servant* reigns, and when a fool is filled with food;
and a hated (woman) is married,
and when a maid is heir to her mistress.
—   Prov. 30:21-23

Poverty and wealth

*The following verses discuss both poverty and wealth. See separate
categories for poverty and wealth below. In the following, the
Hebrew word used for poverty is* רֵישׁ *(resh) except where
indicated.*

One who deals with a slack hand becomes poor,
but the hand of the hard workers becomes rich.
—   Prov. 10:4

Wealth of the rich is his strength of the city,
the ruin of the weak is their poverty.
—   Prov. 10:15 (דַּל dl)

There is who is scattering, and yet is increased,
 And who is keeping back from uprightness, only to want.
—   Prov. 11:24

There is one acting rich who has not at all,
one acting poor has much capital.

The ransom of a man's (אִישׁ ish) life is his riches,
but the poor does not hear a rebuke.
— Prov. 13:7-8

Even by his neighbor the poor is hated,
but lovers of the rich are many.
— Prov. 14:20

A poor man uses entreaties,
but the rich answer roughly.
— Prov. 18:23

Wealth brings many new friends,
but the weak is deserted by his friend.
— Prov. 19:4 (דַּל dl)

A man (אִישׁ ish) who loves joy will be poor (מַחְסוֹר),
he who loves wine and oil will not be rich.
— Prov. 21:17

The rich and the poor meet together,
the Lord is maker of them all.
— Prov. 22:2

The rich rules over the poor,
— Prov. 22:7a

He who oppresses the poor to increase his own wealth,
or gives to the rich, will only come to need (מַחְסוֹר).
— Prov. 22:16

(From King Hezekiah's scribes)
Better is the poor who walks in his integrity
than the crooked in his ways even if rich.
— Prov. 28:6

A rich man (אִישׁ ish) is wise in his own eyes,
but a poor one who has understanding will find him out.
— Prov. 28:11 דַּל (dal)

A man (אִישׁ ish) with an evil eye hastens after capital
and knows not that want will come upon him.
— Prov. 28:22

(From Agur of Massa)
Two things I ask of thee;
deny them not to me before I die:
Vanity and the word of a lie remove far from me
poverty and riches do not give to me,
lest I be full and deny thee
and say, "Who is the Lord (יהוה Yahweh)?"
or lest I be poor, and steal,
and profane the name of my God (אֱלֹהִים Elohim).
— Prov. 30:7-9

poverty רֵישׁ (resh) (no modern usage)

This word is used in the Hebrew Bible only in the The Proverbs.

So shall your *poverty* come as one stalking,
and your want as a shield of man (אִישׁ ish).
— Prov. 6:11

Poverty and shame come to one who ignores discipline,
— Prov. 13:18a

The fallow ground of the *poor* yields much food,
but it is swept away by injustice.
— Prov. 13:23

He who mocks the *poor* reviles his maker,
he who rejoices at calamity shall not be acquitted.
— Prov. 17:5

Better is a *poor* one who walks in his integrity
than one who is twisted in his speech and is a fool.
—   Prov. 19:1

All the brothers of a *poor* one hate him,
how much more do his friends go far from him!
He pursues them with words but does not have them.
—   Prov. 19:7

and it is better to be a poor one than a man (אִישׁ ish) of a lie.
—   Prov. 19:22

Love not sleep, lest you become *poor,*
open your eyes and you will have plenty of bread.
—   Prov. 20:13

A little sleep, a little slumber,
a little folding of the hands to rest,
and *poverty* will come upon you like a robber,
and want like an armed man (אִישׁ ish).
—   Prov. 24:33-34

(From Hezekiah's scribes)
A virile man (גֶּבֶר gbr), poor and oppressing the *poor,*
is a sweeping rain that leaves no food.
—   Prov. 28:3

Better is the *poor* walking in his integrity,
than the perverse of ways who is rich.
—   Prov. 28:6

He who tills his land will have plenty of bread,
but he who follows vanities will have plenty of *poverty.*
—   Prov. 28:19

He who gives to the *poor* will not want,
but he who hides his eyes will get many a curse.

—   Prov. 28:27

The *poor* and a man (אִישׁ ish) of injuries (RSV: oppressor) meet together
the Lord (יהוה Yahweh) enlightens the eyes of both of them.
—   Prov. 29:13

(From Agur of Massa)
Two things I ask of thee;
deny them not to me before I die:
Vanity and the word of a lie remove far from me
poverty and riches do not give to me,
lest I be full and deny thee
and say, "Who is the Lord (יהוה Yahweh)?"
or lest I be poor, and steal,
and profane the name of my God (אֱלֹהִים Elohim).
—   Prov. 30:7-9

(From King Lemuel of Massa)
Give strong drink to him who is perishing,
and wine to those in bitter distress;
let them drink and forget their *poverty*,
and remember their misery no more.
—   Prov. 31:6-7

low, weak, humble דַּל (del) (modern: poor)

*"Pray, Lord, how can I deliver Israel? Behold, my clan is the
weakest in Manasseh, and I am the least in my family," Gideon
said in protesting to the Lord his appointment as a judge. Judges
6:15.*

The poverty of the *weak* is their ruin.
—   Prov. 10:15b

One oppressing the *weak* curses his maker,

218

but he who favors the destitute honors Him.
—   Prov. 14:31

The Lord (יהוה Yahweh) lends to the one favoring the *weak,*
and He will reward his dealing.
—   Prov. 19:17

He who closes his ear to the cry of the *weak*
will himself cry out and not be heard.
—   Prov. 21:13

The eye of the good – he will be blessed,
for he gives bread to the *weak.*
—   Prov. 22:9

He who oppresses the *weak* to increase his own wealth,
or gives to the rich, will only come to want.
—   Prov. 22:16

Do not rob the *weak,* because he is weak,
or crush the afflicted at the gate;
for the Lord will plead their cause and despoil of life those who
despoil them.
—   Prov. 22:22-23

(From King Hezekiah's scribes)
The legs of the lame are *weak,*
—   Prov. 26:7

A virile man (גבר gabor), poor and who oppresses the *weak*
is a sweeping rain that leaves no food.
—   Prov. 28:3

He who augments his wealth by interest and usury
gathers it for the pitier of the *weak.*
—   Prov. 28:8

A growling lion, and a ranging bear,
is the wicked ruler over a *weak* people.
—   Prov. 28:15

The righteous knows the plea of the *weak*;
—   Prov. 29:6b-7a

A king who judges the *weak* with truth
his throne shall be established forever.
—   Prov. 29:14

    <u>humble, afflicted</u>   עָנִי ('oni) (modern: humble, modest)

*The Lord said he had seen the affliction, or humbleness, of his
people in Egypt, Ex. 3:7, 17*

but happy is he who favors the *humble*.
—   Prov. 14:21b

All the days of the *humble* are evil,
—   Prov. 15:15

Better is lowness of spirit with the *humble,*
Than to apportion spoil with the proud.
—   Prov. 16:19

Do not rob the weak, because he is weak,
or crush the *humble* at the gate;
for the Lord (יהוה Yahweh) will plead their cause and despoil of
life those who despoil them.
—   Prov. 22:22-23

(From Agur of Massa)
There are those who curse their fathers
and do not bless their mothers.
There are those who are pure in their own eyes
but are not cleansed of their filth.

There are those – how lofty are their eyes,
how high their eyelids lift!
There are those whose teeth are swords, whose teeth are knives,
to devour the *humble* from off the earth,
the needy from among persons (אָדָם adam).
— Prov. 30:11-14

(From King Lemuel f Massa)
It is not for kings, O Lemuel,
it is not for kings to drink wine,
or for rulers to desire strong drink;
lest they drink and forget what has been decreed,
and pervert the rights of all the *humble*.
— Prov. 31:4-5

Open your mouth, judge righteously,
and defend the *humble* and the destitute.
— Prov. 31:9

    need, deficiency מַחְסוֹר (makhsor) (modern: shortage, want)

A squad of five scouts from the tribe of Dan reported they had found a land "where there is no lack of anything," Judges 18:10.

So shall your poverty come as one stalking,
and your *need* as a shield of man (אִישׁ ish).
— Prov. 6:11

There is who is scattering, and yet is increased,
And who is keeping back from uprightness, only to *need*.
— Prov. 11:24

In all work there is advantage,
but a thing of the lips (i.e., talk) is only to *need*
— Prov. 14:23.

The purposes of the diligent lead only to advantage,
 And of every hasty one, only to *need*.
— Prov. 21:5

Whoso loving mirth is a *needy* man (אִישׁ ish),
— Prov. 21:17

He who oppresses the weak to increase his own wealth,
or gives to the rich, will only come to *need*.
— Prov. 22:16

A little sleep, a little slumber,
a little folding of the hands to rest,
and poverty will come upon you like a robber,
and *need* like an armed man (אִישׁ ish).
— Prov. 24:33-34

(From King Hezekiah's scribes)
He who gives to the poor will not be *needy*,
but he who hides his eyes will get many a curse.
— Prov. 28:27

destitute, needy, poor אֶבְיוֹן (`evyon) (modern: pauper, beggar)

The Lord God told the Israelites to leave their land fallow on the seventh year so the destitute could eat, Ex. 23:11.

He who oppresses a weak one curses his maker,
but he who favors the *destitute* honors Him.
— Prov. 14:31

(From King Lemuel of Massa)
Open your mouth, judge righteously,
and defend the humble and the *destitute*.
— Prov. 31:9

She puts her hand to the poor,

and reaches out her hands to the *destitute*.
—   Prov. 31:20

riches, wealth עֹשֶׁר ('osher) (modern: tithe, enrich)

Abraham referred to himself as wealthy, Gen. 14:23. King Solomon had more wealth than any other king, I Kings 3:13 and 10:23.

Length of days is in her (wisdom's) right (hand),
and in her left, *wealth* and honors.
—   Prov. 3:16

Wealth and honor are with me,
enduring substance and prosperity.
My fruit is better than gold, even fine gold,
and my yield than choice silver.
—   Prov. 8:18-19

Poor *is* he who is working — a slothful hand,
And the hand of the diligent maketh *wealth*.
—   Prov. 10:4

The blessing of the Lord makes *wealth*,
and he adds no sorrow with it.
—   Prov. 10:22

terrifying ones hold to *wealth*.
—   Prov. 11:16b

One trusting in his *wealth* will fall,
—   Prov. 11:28a

The crown of the wise is their *wealth*,
—   Prov. 14:24a

A name is to be chosen than great *wealth*,

and grace is better than silver or gold.
— Prov. 22:1

The reward of humility is fear of the Lord,
wealth and honor and life.
— Prov. 22:4

Do not toil to be w*ealthy*; be wise enough to desist.
When your eyes light upon it, it is gone;
for suddenly it takes to itself wings,
flying like an eagle toward heaven.
— Prov. 23:4-5

(From King Hezekiah's scribes)
A faithful man (אִישׁ ish) will abound with blessings,
but he who hastens to be *wealthy* will not go unpunished.
— Prov. 28:20

treasure אוֹצָר (`otsar) (modern: treasure)

Frequently this word refers to place to store treasure as well as the treasue itself. The Lord promised that if the Israelites followed his commandments, he would open up his treasury, the heavens, to provide rain, Deut.28:12.

To cause my lovers to inherit substance,
 Yea, their *treasures* I fill.
— Prov. 8:21 *(wisdom is speaking)*

Treasures gained by wickedness do not profit,
— Prov. 10:2a

Better is a little with the fear of the Lord,
than great *treasure* and tumult with it.
— Prov. 15:16

The getting of *treasures* by a lying tongue

is a fleeting vapor and a snare of death.
—   Prov. 21:6

wealth, riches, capital הוֹן (hon) (modern: capital, wealth)

All capital we find,
we fill our houses *with* spoil,
—   Prov. 1:13

Honor the Lord (Yahweh) with your *capital*,
—   Prov. 3:9a

Wealth and honor are with me,
Capital and righteousness.
—   Prov. 8:18

The *capital* of the rich *is* his strong city,
 The ruin of the poor *is* their poverty.
—   Prov. 10:15 *(see Prov. 18:11 below)*

Capital does not profit in the day of wrath,
—   Prov. 11:4

And the *capital* of a diligent person (אָדָם adam) is precious.
—   Preov. 12:27

There is one acting rich who has not at all,
one acting poor has much *capital*.
—   Prov. 13:7

Capital from vanity will dwindle,
but one gathering by hand shall increase.
—   Prov. 13:11

A rich man's *capital* is his strong city
and like a high wall in his imagination.
—   Prov. 18:11 *(see Prov. 10:15 above)*

A house and *capital* are the legacy of fathers,
but a woman who acts wisely is from the Lord (יהוה Yahweh).
—   Prov. 19:14

And by knowledge the rooms will be filled
with all *capital* precious and pleasant.
—   Prov. 24:4

(From King Hezekiah's scribes)
He who augments his *capital* by interest and usury
gathers it for the pitier of the poor.
—   Prov. 28:8

A man (אִישׁ ish) with an evil eye hastens after *capital*,
and does not know that want will come upon him.
—   Prov. 28:22

but a friend of whores wastes *capital*.
—   Prov. 29:3b

<u>also</u>

One who is good leaves an inheritance to the sons of his sons,
but the sinner's wealth is laid up for the righteous.
—   Prov. 13:22a (חַיִל) (chayil) *(This word generally means strength, force, army and rarely, wealth)*

(From King Hezekiah's scribes)
for riches do not last forever,
and does a crown endure to all generations?
—   Prov. 27:24 (חַיִל)

<u>Work and work habits</u>

One who deals with a slack hand becomes poor,

226

but the hand of the hard workers becomes rich.
— Prov. 10:4

In all work there is profit,
but mere talk tends only to poverty.
— Prov. 14:23

Even by his acts a boy makes himself known,
whether his work is clean and upright.
— Prov. 20:11

The plans of the hard worker lead surely to abundance,
but every one who is hasty comes only to need.
— Prov. 21:5

but as for the pure, his work is upright.
— Prov. 21:8

If you say, "Behold, we did not know this,"
does not he who weighs the hearts perceive it?
Does not the Keeper of your soul should know,
and will he not repay each person (אָדָם adam) according to his
work?
— Prov. 24:12

Do not say, as he has done to me I will do to him,
I will repay each man (אִישׁ ish) according to his work.
— Prov. 24:29

lazy, sluggard) עָצֵל ('atsel) (modern: lazy)

*The five scouts from Dan warned against being lazy – i.e., slow –
in taking the land, Judges 18:9.*

Go to the ant, O *lazy* one,
consider her ways, and be wise.

Without having any chief, officer or ruler,
she prepares her food in the summer,
and gathers her sustenance in harvest.
How long will you lie there, O *lazy* one?
When will you arise from your sleep?
A little sleep, a little slumber,
a little folding of the hands to rest,
and poverty will come upon like a vagabond.
—   Prov. 6:6-11

Like vinegar to the teeth, and smoke to the eyes,
so is the *lazy* one to those who send him.
—   Prov. 10:26

Craving but not getting is the soul of the *lazy* one,
but the soul of hard workers will get fat.
—   Prov. 13:4

The hedge of the *lazy* has thorns,
—   Prov. 15:19a

The *lazy* one buries his hand in the dish,
and will not even bring it back to his mouth.
—   Prov. 19:24

The *lazy* does not plow in the autumn,
he will seek at harvest and have nothing.
—   Prov. 20:4

The lust of the *lazy* one kills him
for his hands refuse to labor.
—   Prov. 21:25

The *lazy* one says, "There is a lion outside! I shall be slain in the
streets."
—   Prov. 22:13 *(see Prov. 26:13)*

I passed by the field of a *lazy* one,
by the vineyard of a man without sense;
and lo, it was all overgrown with thorns;
the ground was covered with nettles,
and its stone wall was broken down.
Then I saw and considered it;
I looked and received instruction.
A little sleep, a little slumber,
a little folding of the hands to rest,
and poverty will come upon you like a robber,
and want like an armed man.
— Prov. 24:30-34

(From King Hezekiah's scribes)
The *lazy* one says,
"There is a lion in the road! There is a lion in the streets!"
As a door turns on its hinges,
so does a lazy one on his bed.
The lazy one buries his hand in the dish;
it wears him out to bring it back to his mouth.
The lazy one is wiser in his own eyes
than seven that return a wise answer.
— Prov. 26:13-16

   slothfully, deceitfully רְמִיָּה (ramiyah) (modern: deceit, cheating)

Jeremiah wrote that cursed is the one doing the work of the Lord slothfully, 28:10.

A *slothful* hand causes poverty,
but the hand of the diligent makes rich.
A son who gathers in summer is prudent,
but a son who sleeps in harvest brings shame.
— Prov. 10:4-5

The hand of the hard workers will rule,

while the *slothful* will be put into forced labor.
—   Prov. 12:24

A *slothful* will not catch his prey,
but a hard-working person (אָדָם adam) will get precious wealth.
—   Prov. 12:27

Sloth casts into a deep sleep,
and an idle person will suffer hunger.
—   Prov. 19:15

Occupation, business מְלָאכָה (modern: work, closely related to
word for artificial)

The Hebrew word, like the modern, is closely related to artificial.
Prov. 18:9 is one of the few instances of this word being used
negatively.

He who is *remiss* in his work is a brother to him who destroys.
—   Prov. 18:9

Do you see a man (אִישׁ ish) skilled (or prompt) in his *occupation*?
He will stand before kings, he will not stand before the obscure.
—   Prov. 22:29

Prepare your work outside,
get everything ready for you in the field;
and after that build your house.
—   Prov. 24:27

 also:
Love not sleep, lest you become a poor man,
open your eyes and you will have plenty of bread.
—   Prov. 20:13

     wages, to hire, to rent שָׂכָר (sekher) (modern: wages,
salary, pay)

A wicked one earns deceptive *wages*,
but one who sows righteousness gets a true reward.
—   Prov. 11:18

Business practices

property

Drink water from your own cistern,
flowing water from your own well.
Should your springs be scattered abroad,
streams of water in the streets?
Let them be for yourself alone,
and not for strangers with you.
—   Prov. 5:15-17

honesty
(See also "Honest" in Chapter 4: Godly Traits.)

A false balance is an abomination to the Lord,
but a just weight is his delight.
—   Prov. 11:1

He who is greedy of gain troubles his house,
but he who hates bribes will live.
—   Prov. 15:27

A scale and balance of justice are to the Lord,
his work is all the weights of the bag.
—   Prov. 16:11

A stone and a stone (RSV: diverse weights and balances) are
both alike an abomination onto the Lord (יְהוָֹה Yahweh).
—   Prov. 20:10

A stone and a stone (RSV: diverse weights) are an abomination to
the Lord (יְהוָֹה Yahweh),

and deceitful scales are not good.
— Prov. 20:23

Borrowing, lending (surety, guarantor) עֲרַב ('arav) (modern: guarantor, warrantor)

This word is closely related to the Hebrew word for sweet or sunset, of which there are many more uses in the Hebrew Bible and the Proverbs.

My son, if you are *surety* for your neighbor,
if you struck with a stranger,
are you snared with the words of your mouth
are you captured with the words of mouth?
— Prov. 6:1-2

One suffers evil when he is *surety* for an alien,
but he who hates *surety* is secure.
— Prov. 11:14

He who gives *surety* for a stranger will suffer evil,
but he who hates *suretyship* is secure.
— Prov. 11:15

A person (אָדָם adam) lacking heart is striking hands,
A *surety* he becometh before his friend.
— Prov. 17:18

Take one's garment when he has given *surety* for a stranger,
and hold him in pledge when he gives *surety* for aliens.
— Prov. 20:16 *(compare Prov. 27:13 below)*

and the borrower is slave to the man (אִישׁ ish) who lends.
— Prov. 22:7b

Be not one of those who gives pledges, who become *surety* for debts.

If you nothing with which to pay, why should your bed be taken
from under you?
— Prov. 22:26-27

Take his garment that is *surety* for a stranger,
and take a pledge of him for a strange woman.
— Prov. 27:13 *(see Prov. 20:16 above)*

buying and selling

The people will curse him who holds back grain,
but a blessing is on the head of him who sells it.
— Prov. 11:26

"It is evil, it is evil," says the buyer,
but when he goes away he boasts.
— Prov. 20:14

Inheritance, possession, property נַחֲלָה (nahalah) (modern:
heritage, estate)

The Lord God spoke repeatedly of giving Israel the Promised Land
as an inhritance, Deut. 4:20, 4:38, 15:4, 20:16, 21:23, 25:19,
26:1.

A good one leaves an *inheritance* to the sons of his sons,
— Prov. 13:22a

In the fear of the Lord (יהוה Yahweh) is strong confidence,
and to his sons shall be a hiding place.
— Prov. 14:26a

A wise servant ruleth over a son causing shame,
 And in the midst of brethren he shares an *inheritance*.
— Prov. 17:2

A house and capital are the legacy of fathers,

but a woman who acts wisely is from the Lord (יהוה Yahweh).
—   Prov. 19:14

An *inheritance* gotten hastily in the beginning will in the end not
be blessed.
—   Prov. 20:21

Lottery גּוֹרָל (gora) (modern: destiny, fate, lot, luck)

*Lot was used extensively in the early history of Israel for the
apportionment of property as well as the family estate.*

Thy *lot* thou dost cast among us,
one purse is — to all of us.'
—   Prov. 1:14

Into the centre is the *lot* cast,
and from the Lord (יהוה Yahweh) is all its judgment.
—   Prov. 16:33

The *lot* puts an end to contention
and decides among the mighty.
—   Prov. 18:18

Farming

Honor the Lord with your substance
and with the first fruits of all your produce;
then your barns will be filled with plenty,
and your vats will be bursting with wine.
—   Prov. 3:9-10

Drink water from your own cistern,
flowing water from your own well.
Should your springs be scattered abroad,
streams of water in the streets?
Let them be for yourself alone,

and not for strangers with you.
Let your fountain be blessed...
—   Prov. 5:15-18a

The fallow ground of the poor yields much food,
but it is swept away by injustice.
—   Prov. 13:23

Where there are no oxen, there is no grain;
but abundant crops come by the strength of the oxen.
—   Prov. 14:4

The lazy does not plow in the autumn,
he will seek at harvest and have nothing.
—   Prov. 20:4

Prepare your work outside,
get everything ready for you in the field;
and after that build your house.
—   Prov. 24:27

(From King Hezekiah's scribes)
Know well the condition of your flocks,
and give attention to your herds;
for riches do not last forever,
and does a crown endure to all generations?
When the grass is gone, and the new growth appears,
and the herbiage of the mountains is gathers,
the lambs will provide your clothing,
and the goats the price of a field;
there will be enough goats' milk for your food,
for the food of your household
and maintenance for your maidens.
—   Prov. 27:23-28

He who tills his land will have plenty of bread,

but he who follows vanities will have plenty of poverty.
—   Prov. 28:19

For pressing milk produces curds,
pressing the nose produces blood,
and pressing anger brings forth wrath.
—   Prov. 30:33

Chapter 8: POLITICAL MATTERS

Political justice and injustice

    to judge, to administer justice שָׁפַט (shafat) (modern: judge, referee)

This is the word used as the title of the charismatic leaders of the Book of Judges – Gideon, Samson, Jephthah, Deborah, et al — who saved Israel.

By me do chiefs rule, and nobles,
all *judges* of the earth.
—   Prov. 8:16

    justice, judgment מִשְׁפָּט (mishpat) (modern: judgment))
See entry in Chapter X: "Principles," and "Economic Violence and Oppression," in Chapter VII: "Economic Matters."

Samuel's sons took bribes and perverted justice, I Samuel 8:3.

The fallow ground of the poor yields much food,
but it is swept away by no *justice.*
—   Prov. 13:23

(From King Hezekiah's scribes)
Evil men (אִישׁ ish) do not understand *justice,*
but those seeking the Lord (יהוה Yahweh) understand all.
—   Prov. 28:5

A king by *judgment* establishes a land,
but a man (אִישׁ ish) taking bribes tears it down.
— Prov. 29:4

Many are seeking the face of a ruler,
but from the Lord (יהוה Yahweh) is *judgment* for a man (אִישׁ
ish).
— Prov. 29:26

oppression מַעֲשַׁקּוֹת (m'ashaqqot) (modern: exploit,
subdue, rob)

*"He who walks righteously and speaks uprightly, who despises the
gain of oppressions, who shakes his hands, lest they hold a bribe,
who stops his ears from hearing of bloodshed and shuts his eyes
from looking upon evil, he will dwell on the heights; his place of
defense will be the fortresses of rocks; his bread will be given him,
his water will be sure,"* Isa. 33:15-16. *See also oppression in
Chapter 7: Economic Matters.*

(From King Hezekiah's scribes)
Like a roaring lion and a charging bear
is a wicked ruler over weak people.
A prince who lacks understanding is a cruel *oppressor*;
but he who hates unjust gain will prolong his days.
— Prov. 28:15-16

violence חָמָס (hamas) (modern: corruption, violence)

*Prior to the flood, the earth was corrupt before God and filled with
violence, Gen. 6:11.*

For they eat the bread of wickedness
and drink the wine of *violence*.
— Prov. 4:17

but the wicked's covers *violence.*
—   Prov. 10:6b, 10:11b

but the soul of the traitor eats *violence.*
—   Prov. 13:2

A man (אִישׁ ish) of *violence* entices his neighbor
and leads him in a way that is not good.
—   Prov. 16:29

also:

Rescue those who are being taken away to death;
hold back those who are stumbling to the slaughter.
—   Prov. 24:11

(From King Hezekiah's scribes)
Like a roaring lion and a charging bear is a wicked ruler over weak
people.
—   Prov. 28:15

violence, havoc, destruction שׁד (shod) (no modern
definition)

The biblical word is similar to a similar biblical and modern word
for demon or devil. A similar word is used throughout the Hebrew
Bible for a woman's breast. "Wail, for the day of the Lord is near;
as havoc from the Almighty it will come!" Isa. 13:6.

The *havoc* of the wicked ensnares them
because they refuse to do what is just.
—   Prov. 21:7

Be not envious of evil men (אִישׁ ish), nor desire to be with them;
for their minds devise *havoc* and their lips talk of mischief.
—   Prov. 24:1-2

violent, terrible, ruthless עָרִיץ ('arits) (modern: despot, tyrant)

"I will punish the world for its evil, and the wicked for their iniquity; I will put an end to the pride of the arrogant, and lay low the haughtiness of the ruthless," Isa. 13:11.

and the *ruthless* get riches.
—   Prov. 11:16b

War מִלְחָמָה (milhamah) (modern: war, battle)

Plans are established by counsel,
by guidance wage *war*.
—   Prov. 20:18

A wise one scales the city of the mighty
and topples the force in which they trust.
—   Prov. 21:22

The horse is made ready for the day of *war*,
but deliverance (belongs) to the Lord (יהוה Yahweh).
—   Prov. 21:31

A wise warrior (גֶּבֶר gbr) strengthens himself,
a man (אִישׁ ish) of knowledge firms up strength;

For by wise guidance you can wage your *war*,
and in abundance of counselors there is victory.
—   Prov. 24:5-6

Those in authority

king מֶלֶךְ (melekh) (modern: king, ruler)

(Modern Israelis chant, "Ariel Hamalek! Ariel Hamalek," in reference to their prime minister.)

By me *kings* reign,
and princes decree what is righteous;
by me rulers rule,
and nobles judge the earth.
—   Prov. 8:15-16 *(wisdom is speaking)*

In the multitude of people is the honor of a *king*,
but without people a prince is ruined.
—   Prov. 14:28

Righteousness exalts a nation,
but sin is a reproach to any people.
A servant who deals wisely has the *king*'s favor,
but his wrath falls on one who acts shamefully.
—   Prov. 14:34-35

Inspired decisions are on the lips of the *king*,
his mouth does not sin in justice.
—   Prov. 16:10

It is an abomination to kings to commit wickedness,
for the throne is established by righteousness.
Righteous lips are the delight of *kings*,
and he loves him who speaks uprightly.
A *king*'s fury is a messenger of death,
and a wise man (אִישׁ ish) will cover it.
In the light of a *king*'s face there is life,
and his favor is like the clouds that bring spring rain.
—   Prov. 16:12-15

Like a lion's roar is a *king*'s rage,
but his favor is like dew upon the grass.
—   Prov. 19:12

Like a lion's roar is the dread of a *king*,
he who provokes him to anger sins against his own soul (forfeits his life).
—   Prov. 20:2

A *king* who sits on the throne of judgment
winnows all evil with his eyes.
—   Prov. 20:8

A wise *king* winnows the wicked,
and drives the wheel over them.
—   Prov. 20:26

Mercy and truth preserve the *king*,
and his throne is upheld by mercy.
—   Prov. 20:28

As the waters of streams,
a *king's* heart is in the hands of the Lord (יהוה Yahweh),
wherever He desires he inclines it.
—   Prov. 21:1

One who loves purity of heart, and grace is on his lips,
will have the *king* as his friend.
—   Prov. 22:11

Do you see a man (אִישׁ ish) skilled (or prompt) in his occupation?
He will stand before *kings*, he will not stand before the obscure.
—   Prov. 22:29

Fear the Lord (יהוה Yahweh), my son, and the king,
and do not associate with those who change,
for suddenly their woe shall rise,
and who knows the ruin that will come from them both?
—   Prov. 24:21-22

(From King Hezekiah's scribes)
It is the glory of God (אֱלֹהִים Elohim) to conceal things,
but the glory of *kings* is to search things out.
As the heavens for height, and the earth for depth,
so the heart of *kings* is unsearchable.
Take away the dross from the silver,
and the smith has material for a vessel;
take away the wicked from the presence of the *king*,
and his throne will be established in righteousness.
Do not put yourself forward in the *king*'s presence,
or stand in the place of the great;
for it is better to be told, "Come up here,"
than to be put lower in the presence of a prince.
—   Prov. 25:1-6

A *king* by justice establishes a land,
but a man (אִישׁ ish) taking bribes tears it down.
—   Prov. 29:4

A *king* who judges the poor with truth
his throne shall be established forever.
—   Prov. 29:14

(From Agur of Massa)
Under three things the earth trembles; under four it cannot bear up:
For a servant when he *reigneth*,
and a fool when he is satisfied with bread,
for a hated one when she ruleth, And a maid-servant when she
succeedeth her mistress.
—   Prov. 30:21-23

A *king* there is not to the locust, And it goeth out — each one
shouting,
the lizard you can take in your hands, yet it is in *kings'* palaces.
—   Prov. 30:27-28

Three things are stately in their tread;
four are stately in their stride;
the lion, which is the mightiest among the beasts
and does not turn back before any;
the strutting cock, the he-goat,
and a *king* striding before his people.
— Prov. 30:29-31

(From King Lemuel of Massa)
Not for *kings*, O Lemuel, Not for *kings*, to drink wine,
 And for princes a desire of strong drink.
— Prov. 31:4

     prince שַׂר (sar) (modern: minister, head, chief)

*In the account of Deborah and Barak, Sisera is identified as the
prince, or commander, of Jabin's army, Judges 5:14*

By me do *princes rule*, and nobles,
 all judges of the earth.
— Prov. 6:7

It is ... much less (fitting) for a slave to rule over *princes*.
— Prov. 19:10

(From King Hezekiah's scribes)
When a land transgresses it has many *princes*;
but by a discerning person (אָדָם adam) who knows, it is
prolonged.
— Prov. 28:2

(From King Lemuel of Massa)
Not for kings, O Lemuel, Not for kings, to drink wine,
 and for *princes* a desire of strong drink.
— Prov. 31:4

ruler מֹשֵׁל (moshel) (modern: ruler, governor)

Go unto the ant, O slothful one, See her ways and be wise;
which has not captain, dictator, and *ruler,*
—   Prov. 6:6-7

The hand of the diligent *rules*
—   Prov. 12:24a

One who is slow to anger is better than he who is mighty,
and one who *rules* his spirit than he who takes a city.
—   Prov. 16:32

A slave who deals wisely will *rule* over a son who acts shamefully,
—   Prov. 17:2

It is ... much less (fitting) for a slave to *rule* over princes.
—   Prov. 19:10

When you sit down to eat with a *ruler,*
observe carefully what is before you;
and put a knife to your throat if you are a possessor of appetite.
Do not desire his delicacies for it is the bread of lies.
—   Prov. 23:1-3

(From King Hezekiah's scribes)
Like a roaring lion and a charging bear
is a wicked *ruler* over poor people.
A *ruler* who lacks understanding is a cruel oppressor;
but he who hates unjust gain will prolong his days.
—   Prov. 28:15

When the righteous increase, the people rejoice;
but when the wicked *rule,* the people groan.
—   Prov. 29:2

A *ruler* who listens to a false word,
all his ministers are wicked.
— Prov. 29:12

Many are seeking the face of a *ruler*,
but from the Lord (יהוה Yahweh) is justice for a man (אִישׁ ish).
— Prov. 29:26

dictator, ruler קָצִין (qatsin) (modern: officer)

The people of Gilead asked Judge Jephthah to become their dictator, Judges 11.

Go unto the ant, O slothful one, See her ways and be wise;
which has not captain, *dictator,* and ruler,
— Prov. 6:6-7

By long-suffering is a *dictator* persuaded,
— Prov. 25:15a

messenger מַלְאָךְ (maal`akh) (modern: officer)

A wicked *messenger* plunges into evil,
but a faithful ambassador is healing.
— Prov. 13:17

The fury of a king is *messengers* of death,
— Prov. 16:14a

A rebel seeks evil,
and so a cruel *messenger* will be sent against him.
— Prov. 17:11

ambassador צִיר (tsir) (modern: delegate, messenger)

*The people of Gibeon went to Joshua at Gilgal and feigned to be
ambassadors, Josh. 9:4*

A wicked messenger plunges into evil,
but a faithful *ambassador* is healing.
—   Prov. 13:17

(From King Hezekiah's scribes)
Like the cold of snow in the time of harvest is a faithful
ambassado to those who send him,
he refreshes the spirit of his masters.
—   Prov. 25:13

Chapter 9: NATURE

<u>Creation</u>

The Lord (יהוה Yahweh) by wisdom founded the earth;
by understanding he established the heavens;
by his knowledge the deeps broke forth,
and the clouds drop down the dew.
—   Prov. 3:19-20

The Lord (יהוה Yahweh) created me at the beginning of his
work,
the first of his acts of old.
Ages ago I was set up,
at the first, before the beginning of the earth.
When there were no depths I was brought forth,
when there were no springs abounding with water,
Before the mountains had been shaped,
before the hills, I was brought forth;
before he had made the earth with its fields,
or the first of the dust of the world,
When he established the heavens, I was there,
when he drew a circle of the face of the deep,
when he made firm the skies above,
when he established the fountains of the deep,
when he assigned to the sea its limit,
so that the waters might not transgress his command,
when he marked out the foundations of the earth,
then I was beside him, like a master workman;
and I was daily his delight,
rejoicing before him always,

rejoicing in his inhabited world
and delighting in the sons of men.
—   Prov. 8:23-31

(From King Hezekiah's scribes)
As the heavens for height, and the earth for depth,
so the mind of kings is unsearchable.
—   Prov. 25:3

(From Agur of Massa)
Who has ascended to heaven and come down?
Who has gathered the wind in his fist?
Who has established all the ends of the earth?
What is his name, and what is his son's name?
Surely you know!
—   Prov. 30:4

Water מַיִם (mayim)

See also Creation, above.

Drink *water* from your own cistern, flowing *water* from your own well.
Let thy fountains be scattered abroad,
in broad places rivulets of *waters*.
—   Prov. 5:15-16

Stolen waters are sweet,
—   Prov. 9:17 *(quoting the foolish woman talking to a man without sense)*

Like the releasing of *water* is the beginning of strife,
—   Prov. 17:14a

The words of a man's (אִישׁ ish) mouth are deep *waters*,
the fountain of wisdom is a gushing stream.
—   Prov. 18:4

Like deep *water* is counsel in a man's (אִישׁ ish) heart,
but as man (אִישׁ ish) of understanding will draw it out.
—   Prov. 20:5

As the rivers of *waters*,
the king's heart is in the hand of the Lord.
—   Prov. 21:1

(From King Hezekiah's scribes)
If he who hates you does hunger, cause him to eat bread,
And if he thirsts, cause him to drink *water*.
—   Prov. 25:21

Like a fouled spring or a polluted fountain
is the righteous tottering before the wicked.
—   Prov. 25:26

Iron sharpens iron,
and one man (אִישׁ ish) sharpens another.
He who tends a fig tree will eat its fruit,
and he who guards his master will be honored.
As in *water* face answers to face,
so the mind of a person (אָדָם adam) reflects the person (אָדָם adam).
—   Prov. 27:17-19

(From Agur of Massa)
The leech has two daughters; "Give, give," they cry.
Three things are never satisfied; four never say, "Enough":
Sheol, and the barren womb,
the earth not filled with *water*,
and the fire which never says, "Enough."
—   Prov. 30:16b

Birds and animals
-    bird צִפּוֹר (tsifor)
     wings כָּנָף (kagaf) (modern: wing, fender)

ox שׁוֹר (shor) (modern: bull, ox)

For in vain is a net spread in the sight of any *wing*.
—　Prov. 1:17

Save yourself like a gazelle from the hunter,
like a bird from the hand of the fowler.
Go to the ant, O sluggard,
consider her ways, and be wise.
Without having any chief, officer or ruler,
she prepares her food in the summer,
and gathers her sustenance in harvest.
—　Prov. 6:5-8

He goes after her (a whore) at once,
as an ox goes to the slaughter,
or as a fool to the correction of the stocks,
'till a dart strike through his liver,
as a *bird* hasteth to the snare,
—　Prov. 7:22-23a

Where there are no oxen, there is no grain;
but abundant crops come by the strength of the *ox*.
—　Prov. 14:4

Better is a dinner of herbs where love is
than a fatted *ox* and hatred with it.
—　Prov. 15:17

Let a man (אִישׁ ish) meet a bear robbed of cubs than a fool in his
folly.
—　Prov. 17:12

A king's rage is like the roar of a lion,
but his favor is like dew upon the grass.
—　Prov. 19:12

The dread of a king is like the roar of a lion,
he who provokes him to anger sins against his own soul (forfeits
his life).
— Prov. 20:2

for it (riches) will make for itself *wings* like an eagle,
and fly into the heavens.
— Prov. 23:5

(From King Hezekiah's scribes)
Like snow in summer or rain in harvest,
so honor is not fitting for a fool.
Like a *bird* in its flitting, like a swallow in its flying,
a curse that is causeless does not alight.
A whip for the horse, a bridle for the ass,
and a rod for the back of fools.
— Prov. 26:1-3

Like one who grabs the ears of a dog,
is the passerby enraging himself over strife not his.
— Prov. 26:17

As a *bird* wandering from her nest,
so a man (אִישׁ ish) wandering from his place.
— Prov. 27:8

And the righteous as a young lion is confident.
— Prov. 28:1b

(From Agur of Massa)
The leech has two daughters,
"Give, give," they cry.
Three things are never satisfied;
four never say,"Enough!"
Sheol, the barren womb, the earth ever thirsty for water,
and the fire which never says, "Enough."
The eye that mocks a father and scorns to obey a mother

will be picked out by the ravens of the valley
and eaten by the vultures.
Three things are too wonderful for me;
four I do not understand:
the way of an eagle in the sky, the way of a serpant on a rock,
the way of a ship of the high seas,
and the way of a virile man (גֶּבֶר gabor) with a maiden.
—   Prov. 30:15-19

Four things on earth are small, but they are exceedingly wise:
the ants are a people not strong,
yet they provide their food in the summer;
the badgers are a people not mighty,
yet they make their homes in the rocks;
the locusts have no king,
yet all of them march in rank;
the lizard you can take in your hands,
yet it is in kings' palaces.
Three things are stately in their tread;
four are stately in their stride;
the lion, which is the mightiest among the beasts
and does not turn back before any;
the strutting cock, the he-goat,
and a king striding before his people.
—   Prov. 30:24-31

Weather and storms

*The Hebrew word for wind רוּחַ (ruakh) is the same as the word
for spirit.*

I will mock when panic strikes you,
when panic strikes you like a storm,
and your calamity comes like a whirlwind,
when distress and anguish come upon you.
—   Prov. 1:26b-27 (*Wisdom is speaking*)

One troubling his house will inherit the *wind*.
—   Prov. 11:29

and his (a king's) favor is like the clouds of spring rain.
—   Prov. 16:15b

(From King Hezekiah's scribes)
Like the cold of
snow in the time of harvest
is a faithful messenger to those who send him,
he refreshes the spirit of his masters.
Like clouds and wind without rain
is a man (איש ish) who boasts of a gift he does not give.
—   Prov. 25:13-14

The north *wind* brings forth rain;
and a backbiting tongue, angry looks.
—   Prov. 25:23

Like snow in summer or rain in harvest,
so honor is not fitting for a fool.
Like a bird in its flitting, like a swallow in its flying,
a curse tht is causeless does not alight.
A whip for the horse, a bridle for the ass,
and a rod for the back of fools.
—   Prov. 26:1-3

To restrain her (a contentious woman) is to restrain the *wind*
 or to grasp oil in his right hand.
—   Prov. 27:16

(From Agur of Massa)
Who has ascended to heaven and come down?
 Who has gathered the *wind* in his fists?
 Who has wrapped up the waters in a garment?

Who has established all the ends of the earth?
What is his name, and what is his son's name Surely you know!
—   Prov. 30:4

Silver, gold and jewels

If you seek it like silver and search for it as for hidden treasures;
then you will understand the fear of the Lord (יהוה Yahweh) and
find the knowledge of God (אֱלֹהִים Elohim).
—   Prov. 2:4-5

Happy is the person (אָדָם adam) who finds wisdom,
and the person (אָדָם adam) who gets understanding,
for the gain from it is better than gain from silver
and its profit better than gold.
She is more precious than jewels,
and nothing you desire can compare with her.
—   Prov. 3:13-15

Take my discipline instead of silver,
and knowledge rather than choice gold;
for wisdom is better than jewels,
and all that you may desire cannot compare with her.
—   Prov. 8:10-11

Better than gold, pure gold, is my fruit,
and my produce than choice silver.
—   Prov. 8:18

The tongue of the righteous is chosen silver,
 The heart of the wicked — as a little thing.
—   Prov. 10:20

To get wisdom is better than gold,
to get understanding is to be chosen rather than silver.
—   Prov. 16:16

The crucible is for silver, and the furnace is for gold,
and the Lord (יהוה Yahweh) tries hearts.
— Prov. 17:3

There is gold, and abundance of costly stones,
but the lips of knowledge are a precious jewel.
— Prov. 20:15

and better than silver or gold, is grace.
— Prov. 22:1b

Take away the dross from the silver,
and the smith has material for a vessel.
— Prov. 25:4

A word fitly spoken is like apples of gold in a setting of silver,
Like a gold ring or an ornament of gold
is a wise reprover to a listening ear.
— Prov. 25:11-12

Silver of dross spread over potsherd,
are burning lips and an evil heart.
— Prov. 26:23

As the crucible is for silver,
and the furnace is for gold,
so a man (איש ish) to his praise.
— Prov. 27:21

Chapter 10: CITIES

City, town עִיר ('ir) (modern: city, town, urbanized)

The psalmist often refers to the "city of God," 46:5, 48:1, and 87:3, as well as Jerusalem as a city, 122:3. "Unless the Lord watches over the city, the watchman stays awake in vain," Psalm 127:1b, was quoted in the text of John F. Kennedy's final speech..

he who rules his spirit (is better) than one who takes a *city*.
—   Prov. 16:32b

A wise one scales the *city* of the mighty
and topples the force in which they trust.
—   Prov. 21:22

(From King Hezekiah's scribes)
Like a broken down *city* without a wall
is a man (אִישׁ ish) in whom there is not control in his spirit.
—   Prov. 25:28

Town, city קִרְיָה (qiryah) (modern: city, town)

At the side of the gates, at the mouth of the *town*,
the entrance of the openings, she (Wisdom) crieth aloud,
—   Prov. 8:3

She (Wisdom) has sent forth her damsels,
She crieth on the tops of the high places of the *town*:
—   Prov. 9:3

And she hath sat at the opening of her house,
 on a throne — the high places of the *town*.
—   Prov. 9:14

When the righteous prosper, the *town* rejoices,
—   Prov. 11:10a

By the blessing of the upright a *town* is lifted up,
but by the mouth of the wicked it is overthrown.
—   Prov. 11:11

A rich ones wealth is his strong *town*,
 and like a high wall protecting him.
—   Prov. 18:11

A brother helped is like a strong *town*,
—   Prov. 18:19a

(From King Hezekiah's scribes)
Men (אִישׁ ish) of scorn puff against (i.e., set aflame) a *town*.
—   Prov. 29:8a

PART III: PRINCIPLES

Chapter 11: PRINCIPLES

To know wisdom and discipline, understand words of insight,
receive discipline in wise dealing, righteousness, justice, and
uprightness;
that prudence may be given to the simple, knowledge and
discretion to the youth—the wise also may hear and increase in
learning, and the man of understanding acquire skill, to understand
a proverb and a figure, the words of the wise and their riddles.
—   Prov. 1:2-6

Commandments מִצְוָה (mitsvah) (modern: commandment,
precept)

*Interestingly, the Hebrew word is not used to refer to the Ten
Commandments in Ex.20, but rather is used within the second
commandment linked to keeping the Lord God's commandments
and showing mercy* חֶסֶד *(hesed).*

My son, if you receive my words
and hide my *commandments* with you

....

then you will understand the fear of the Lord (יהוה Yahweh)
and find the knowledge of God (אֱלֹהִים Elohim).
—   Prov. 2:1,5

My son, do not forget my law,
but my *commandments* let your heart guard;
for length of days and years of life and peace will they give you.
—   Prov. 3:1-2

And he taught me and said to me,
May my words cling to your heart,
and keep my *commandments* and life.
—   Prov. 4:4

My son, keep your father's *commandment*,
and forsake not your mother's law.
Bind them upon your heart always;
tie them about your neck.
When you walk, they will lead you;
when you lie down, they will watch over you;
and when you awake, they will talk with you.
For the *commandmen*t is a lamp and the teaching a light,
and the corrections of discipline are the way of life,
you from the evil woman,
from the smooth tongue of the adventuress.
—   Prov. 6:20-24

My son, keep my words and treasure up my *commandments*
with you;
keep my *commandments* and live,
and my teachings as the apple of your eye;
bind them on your fingers,
write them on the tablet of your heart.
—   Prov. 7:1-3

but the one who respects the *commandment* will be rewarded.
—   Prov. 13:13b

He who keeps the *commandment* keeps his life,
and he who despises His ways will die.
—   Prov. 19:16

Counsel עֵצָה ('etsah) (modern: advice, counsel)

Jethro provided counsel to Moses, Ex. 18:19.

and you have ignored all my *counsel*
and would have none of my correction,
—   Prov. 1:25

because they hated knowledge and did not choose the fear of the
Lord (יהוה Yahweh),
would have none of my *counsel*,
and despised all my correction,
therefore they shall eat the fruit of their way
and with their own devices be filled.
—   Prov. 1:29-31

To me is *counsel* and sound guidance,
I have insight and strength.
—   Prov. 8:14

When there is no wise guidance, a people falls;
but there is safety in a great *counselor*.
—   Prov. 11:14

The way of a fool is right in his own eyes,
and whoso hearkens to *counsel* is wise.
—   Prov. 12:15

but to the *counselors* of peace is joy.
—   Prov. 12:20b

but with those who take *counsel* is wisdom.
—   Prov. 13:10b

Purposes are frustrated without secret counsel,
but with many *counselors* they succeed.
—   Prov. 15:22 (different Hebrew words)

Consulting (RSV: winking) his eyes to devise froward things,

Moving his lips he has accomplished evil.
—   Prov. 16:30

Hear *counsel* and accept discipline that you may be wise in the end.
Many are the purposes in a man's (אִישׁ ish) heart,
but the *counsel* of the Lord (יהוה Yahweh) will rise (prevail).
—   Prov. 19:20-21

Like deep water is *counsel* in a man's (אִישׁ ish) heart,
—   Prov. 20:5a

Plans are established by *counsel*,
and by wise guidance wage war.
—   Prov. 20:18

There is no wisdom, no understanding, no *counsel* against the Lord.
—   Prov. 21:30

(From King Hezekiah's scribes
Ointment and perfume rejoice the heart,
And sweet is one's friend — from *counsel* of the soul.
—   Prov. 27:9

Guidance, counsel, wisdom תַּחְבּוּלָה (tahbulah) (modern: advice, counsel)

Compare practical wisdom, תּוּשִׁיָּה *(tushiyyah).*

In the absence of wise *guidance* a people falls;
but there is safety in a great counselor.
—   Prov. 11:14

Plans are established by counsel,
and by wise *guidance* wage war.
— Prov. 20:18

For by wise *guidance* you can wage war
and deliverance is by a great counselor.
— Prov. 24:6

Secret counsel סוֹד (sod) (modern: secret)

The secret counsel of the Lord is for those who fear him, Psalms 25:14.

For an abomination to the Lord (יהוה Yahweh) is the perverted,
and with the upright is His *secret counsel.*
— Prov. 3:32

A busybody is revealing secret counsel,
and the faithful of spirit is covering the matter.
— Prov. 11:13   *(Note Prov. 20:19a below)*

Purposes are frustrated without *secret counsel,*
but with many counselors they succeed.
— Prov. 15:22

A revealer of *secret counsels* is the busybody,
— Prov. 20:19a

Discipline

   discipline, reproof, chastisement מוּסָר (musar) (modern: moral, ethics)

English versions sometimes translate this word as "instruction," as in Prov. 13:1 and 18. But mere "instruction" does not capture the force of "discipline."

Discipline of the Lord, my son, do not despise
or be weary of his correction,
for whom the Lord loves he corrects him whom he loves,
as a father the son in whom he delights.
—   Prov. 3:11-12

Hear, ye sons, the *discipline* of a father,
—   Prov. 4:1a

My son, be attentive to my words;
incline your ear to my sayings.
Let them not escape from your sight;
keep them in your heart.
For they are life to him who finds them,
and healing to all his flesh.
—   Prov. 4:20-22

My son, be attentive to my wisdom,
bow your ear to my understanding;
that you may keep discretion,
and your lips may guard knowledge.
—   Prov. 5:1-2

and you groan when the end of your life comes,
when your flesh and body are consumed, and you say,
"How I hated *discipline*, and my heart despised correction!
I did not listen to the voice of my teachers
or incline my ear to my instructions.
I was at the point of utter ruin in the assembled congregation."
—   Prov. 5:11-14

He dies in the absence of *discipline,*
and in great folly he is lost.
—   Prov. 5:23

My son, keep your father's commandment,
and forsake not your mother's law.

Bind them upon your heart always;
tie them about your neck.
When you walk, they will lead you;
when you lie down, they will watch over you;
and when you awake, they will talk with you.
For the commandment is a lamp and the teaching a light,
and the corrections of *discipline* are the way of life,
to preserve you from the evil woman,
from the smooth tongue of the adventuress.
—   Prov. 6:20-24

He is going after her straightway,
as an ox unto the slaughter he cometh,
and as a fetter unto the *chastisement* of a fool,
—   Prov. 7:22

Hear *discipline*, and be wise, and slight not.
—   Prov. 8:33

On the path to life is the one keeping *discipline*
but the one forsaking correction is going astray.
—   Prov. 10:17

The one loving *discipline* is loving knowledge
but the one hating correction is stupid.
—   Prov. 12:1

A wise son heeds his father's *discipline*
—   Prov. 13:1

Poverty and shame for the one ignoring *discipline*,
but one keeping correction shall be honored.
—   Prov. 13:18

He who spares the rod hates his son,
but he who loves him *disciplines* him.
—   Prov. 13:24

A fool despises his father's *discipline*,
but he who heeds correction is shrewd.
—   Prov. 15:5

There is *discipline* for the one fortaking the path,
the one hating correction will die.
—   Prov. 15:10

The ear that heeds the correction of life will abide in wisdom.
He who ignores *discipline* despises his own soul,
but he who heeds correction gains heart.
The fear of the Lord is discipline in wisdom,
—   Prov. 15:31-33a

Discipline your son while there is hope,
do not set your soul on his destruction.
—   Prov. 19:18

Hear counsel and accept *discipline* that you may be wise in the
end.
—   Prov. 19:20

Cease, my son, to hear *discipline*
only to stray from words of knowledge.
—   Prov. 19:27

Folly is bound up in the heart of a boy,
the rod of *discipline* will drive it far from him.
—   Prov. 22:15

Bring in for *discipline* (i.e., apply) your heart and your ears to the
words of knowledge.
Do not withhold from a boy *discipline*
for if you strike him with the rod he will not die.
—   Prov. 23:12-13

Buy truth, and do not sell it;
buy wisdom, *discipline*, and understanding.
—   Prov. 23:23

And I see — I — I do set my heart, I have seen — I have received
discipline,
—   Prov. 24:32

(From King Hezekiah's scribes)
Discipline your son, and it will get you rest,
and it will give you delight.
—   Prov. 29:17

By words a servant is not *disciplined*,
for though he understands, there is no answer.
—   Prov. 29:19

correction, chastisement, reproof תּוֹכַחַת (tokhahath)
(modern: punishment)

"You shall be a reproach and a taunt, a warning and a horror, to
the nations round about you, when I execute judgments on you in
anger and fury, and with furious corrections — I, the LORD, have
spoken," Eze. 5:15, RSV

Turn back at my *correction*,
behold, I will pour out to you my spirit;
I will make known my words to you.
—   Prov. 1:23

and you have ignored all my counsel
and would have none of my *correction*,
—   Prov. 1:25

because they hated knowledge and did not choose the fear of the
Lord,
would have none of my counsel,

and despised all my *correction*,
therefore they shall eat the fruit of their way
and with their own devices be filled.
—   Prov. 1:29-31

Discipline of the Lord (יְהֹוָה Yahweh), my son, do not despise
or be weary of his *correction*,
for whom the Lord (יְהֹוָה Yahweh) loves he corrects him whom
he loves,
as a father the son in whom he delights.
—   Prov. 3:11-12

and you groan when the end of your life comes,
when your flesh and body are consumed, and you say,
"How I hated discipline, and my heart despised *correction*!
I did not listen to the voice of my teachers
or incline my ear to my instructors.
I was at the point of utter ruin in the assembled congregation."
—   Prov. 5:11-14

For a lamp *is* the command, And the law a light,
 And a way of life are *corrections* of instruction,
—   Prov. 6:23

Correct not a scorner, lest he hate thee,
Give *correction* to the wise, and he loveth thee.
—   Prov. 9:8

On the path to life is the one keeping discipline
but the one forsaking *correction* is going astray.
—   Prov. 10:17

The one loving discipline is loving knowledge
but the one hating *correction* is stupid.
—   Prov. 12:1

Poverty and shame for the one ignoring discipline,
but one keeping *correction* shall be honored.
—   Prov. 13:18

A fool despises his father's discipline,
but he who heeds correction is shrewd.
—   Prov. 15:5

Discipline is (seems) evil for the one fortaking the path,
the one hating *correction* will die.
—   Prov. 15:10

A scoffer does not love one who *corrects* him,
—   Prov. 15:12a

The ear that heeds the *correction* of life will abide in wisdom.
He who ignores discipline despises his own soul,
but he who heeds *correction* gains heart.
—   Prov. 15:31-32b

and *correct* one with understanding, he will understand knowledge.
—   Prov. 19:25b

(From King Hezekiah's scribes)
Better is open correction than hidden love.
—   Prov. 27:5

A rod and *correction* give wisdom,
And a youth let away is shaming his mother.
—   Prov. 29:15

Good טוֹב (tov) (modern: good, kind, fair, nice, pleasant)

So you will walk in the way of *good*
—   Prov. 2:20a

And find grace and *good* understanding
in the eyes of God (אֱלֹהִים Elohim) and person (אָדָם adam).
— Prov. 3:4

For *good* (i.e., better) is her merchandise
than the merchandise of silver, And than gold — her increase.
— Prov. 3:14

Do not withhold *good* from those to whom it is due,
when it is in your power to do it.
— Prov. 3:27

For *good* learning I have given to you,
My law forsake not.
— Prov. 4:2

For *good* (i.e., better) is wisdom than rubies,
Yea, all delights are not comparable with it.
— Prov. 8:11

Good (i.e. better) is my fruit than gold, even fine gold,
And mine increase than choice silver.
— Prov. 8:19

The desire of the righteous is only *good,*
— Prov. 11:23

The one seeking *good* early seeks favor,
— Prov. 11:27

One who is good obtains favor from the Lord,
— Prov. 12:2a

Good (i.e., better) is the lightly esteemed who has a servant,
than the self-honoured who lacks bread.
— Prov. 12:9

From the fruit of a man's (אִישׁ ish) mouth he is satisfied with *good*,
— Prov. 12:14a

but a *good* word makes it (a man's (אִישׁ ish) heart) glad.
— Prov. 12:25b

From the fruit of a man's (אִישׁ ish) mouth he eats *good*,
— Prov. 13:2

Good prudence gives grace,
— Prov. 13:15a

but the righteous shall be rewarded with *good*.
— Prov. 13:21b

A good (man) leaves an inheritance to the sons of his sons,
— Prov. 13:22a

and a *good* man (אִישׁ ish) (will be filled) with the fruit of his ways.
— Prov. 14:14b

The evil bow down before the *good*,
— Prov. 14:19a

but truth and mercy follow the devisers of *good*.
— Prov. 14:22b

The tongue of the wise makes knowledge *good*,
— Prov. 15:2a

The eyes of the Lord (יהוה Yahweh) are in every place, keeping watch on the evil and the *good*.
— Prov. 15:3

A joyful heart makes a *good* face,
— Prov. 15:13a

Good (i.e., better) is a little with the fear of the LORD
than great treasure and trouble with it.
Good is a dinner of herbs where love is
than a fatted ox and hatred with it.
— Prov. 15:16-17

and a word in its time, how *good* it is.
— Prov. 15:23

and *good* news makes the bones fat.
— Prov. 15:30b

To get wisdom — how much *good* (i.e., better) than gold,
And to get understanding to be chosen than silver!
— Prov. 16:16

Good (i.e., better) is humility of spirit with the poor,
than to apportion spoil with the proud.
The wise in any matter finds *good*,
and whoso is trusting in the Lord (יהוה Yahweh), O his
happiness.
— Prov. 16:19-20

A man (איש ish) of violence entices his neighbor
and leads him in a way that is not *good*.
— Prov. 16:29

Good (i.e., better) is the slow to anger than the mighty,
And the ruler over his spirit than he who is taking a city.
— Prov. 16:32

Good (i.e., better) is a dry morsel, and rest with it,
than a house full of the sacrifices of strife.
— Prov. 17:1

He who returns evil for *good*,
evil will not depart from his house.
—   Prov. 17:13

One of crooked heart does not find *good*,
—   Prov. 17:20a

Also, to fine the righteous is not *good*,
—   Prov. 17:26a

Acceptance of the face of the wicked (RSV: to be partial) is not
good,
to turn aside the righteous in judgment.
—   Prov. 18:5

Good (i.e., better) is the poor walking in his integrity,
than the perverse in his lips, who is a fool.
Also, without knowledge the soul is not *good*,
and the hasty in feet is sinning.
—   Prov. 19:1-2

he who keeps understanding finds *good*.
—   Prov. 19:8

and deceitful scales are not *good*.
—   Prov. 20:23b

Good (i.,e., better) to sit on a corner of the roof,
Than with a woman of contentions and a house of company.
—   Prov. 21:9

Good (i.e., better) to dwell in a wilderness land,
than with a woman of contentions and anger.
—   Prov. 21:19

A good name is to be chosen rather than great riches,
 and favor is *good* (i.e., better) than silver or gold.
—   Prov. 22:1

The eye of the good – he will be blessed,
for he gives bread to the poor.
—   Prov. 22:9

My son, eat honey, for it is *good*,
 and the drippings of the honeycomb are sweet to your taste.
—   Prov. 24:13

To discern faces (RSV: to be partial) in judgment is not good.
—   Prov. 24:23b

(From King Hezekiah's scribes)
Like cold water to a thirsty soul,
so is good news from a far country.
—   Prov. 25:25

The eating of much honey is not *good*,
nor a searching out of one's own honor — honor.
—   Prov. 25:27

Good (i.e., better) is open reproof than hidden love.
—   Prov. 27:5

Good (i.e., better) is a near neighbour than a brother afar off.
—   Prov. 27:10

And the perfect do inherit *good*
—   Prov. 28:10
To discern faces (i.e., to be partial) is not good,
—   Prov. 28:21

(From King Lemuel of Massa)
She has perceived when her merchandise is *good,*
—   Prov. 31:18

Grace

grace, favor חֵן (hen) (modern: grace, charm, favor)

Noah found grace in the eyes of the Lord, Gen. 6:8, and Abraham
asked if he had found favor with the men of Mamre, Gen. 18:3.

Heed, my son, your father's discipline
and do not forsake your mother's law
for they are an ornament of *grace* for your head
and necklaces for your neck.
—   Prov. 1:9

And find *grace* and good understanding
in the eyes of God (אֱלֹהִים Elohim) and a person (אָדָם adam)
—   Prov. 3:4

(Sound wisdom and discretion) shall be
life to your soul and *grace* to your neck.
—   Prov. 3:22

Toward the scorners he is scornful,
but to the humble he gives *grace.*
—   Prov. 3:34

She (understanding) will give your head a wreath of *grace*
and with a crown of glory she will shield you.
—   Prov. 4:9

A hind of loves, and a roe of *grace!*
Let her loves satisfy you at all times, In her love magnify yourself
continually.
—   Prov. 5:19

A *gracious* woman gets honor,
—   Prov. 11:16a

Good prudence gives *grace*,
—   Prov. 13:15a

but the one honoring Him (his Maker)
graces (i.e., favors) the destitute.
—   Prov. 14:31b

The soul of the wicked desires evil,
(and) finds not *grace* in his neighbor's eyes.
—   Prov. 21:10

and *grace* is better than silver or gold.
—   Prov. 22:1b

One who loves purity of heart and *grace* is on his lips,
his friend is the king.
—   Prov. 22:11

(From King Hezekiah's scribes)
One who reproves a person (אָדָם adam) will find more *grace*
afterward
than he who flatters with the tongue.
—   Prov. 28:23

(From King Lemuel of Massa)
Grace is false and beauty is vain,
a woman who fears the Lord shall be praised.
—   Prov. 31:30

     <u>grace, favor, acceptance</u> רָצוֹן (ratson) (modern: desire, will, wish)

Naphtali had favor and blessing from the lord, Deut. 33:23.

For the one finding me (wisdom) finds life,
and he shall obtain *favor* from the Lord (יהוה Yahweh).
— Prov. 8:35

The lips of the righteous know a thing of *favor*,
— Prov. 10:32

And a perfect weight *is* His *favor*.
— Prov. 11:1b

And the perfect of the way are His *favor*.
— Prov. 11:20

The one seeking good earnestly seeks *favor*,
but evil comes to him who searches for it.
— Prov. 11:27

One who is good obtains *favor* from the Lord (יהוה Yahweh),
— Prov. 12:2a

but among the righteous is *favor*.
— Prov. 14:9

The *favor* of the king is to the servant who acts prudently.
— Prov. 14:35

And the prayer of the upright *is* His *favor*.
— Prov. 15:8

The *favor* of kings is righteous lips
— Prov. 16:13
and his (the king's) is like a cloud of the spring rain.
— Prov. 16:15

He who finds a good wife finds good,
and gets *favor* from the Lord (יהוה Yahweh).
— Prov. 18:22

Justice and injustice

    to judge, to administer justice שָׁפַט (shafat) (modern: judge, referee)

Judgings are prepared for scoffers,
—   Prov. 19:29

A wise man (אִישׁ ish) is *judged* by the foolish man (אִישׁ ish), and he has been angry, and he hath laughed, and there is no rest.
—   Prov. 29:9

    judgment, justice מִשְׁפָּט (mishpat) (modern: judgment, trial, case, sentence)

he is a shield to those who walk in integrity,
guarding the paths of *justice* and preserving the way of his saints,
Then you will understand righteousness and justice and equity,
every good path
—   Prov. 2:7b-9

I walk in the way of righteousness,
in the paths of *justice*,
endowing with wealth those who love me,
and filling their treasuries.
—   Prov. 8:20-21

The thoughts of the righteous are *just*;
—   Prov. 12:5a

The fallow ground of the poor yields much food,
but it is swept away by no *justice*.
—   Prov. 13:23

Better is a little with righteousness
than much increase without *justice*.
—   Prov. 16:8

Inspired decisions are on the lips of the king,
his mouth does not sin in *justice*.
—   Prov. 16:10

A *just* balance and scales are the Lord (יהוה Yahweh)'s,
all the weights in bag are his word.
—   Prov. 16:11

The wicked takes a bribe from the bosom to pervert the ways of
justice.
—   Prov. 17:23

or (it is not good) to deprive a righteous one of *justice*.
—   Prov. 18:5b

A worthless witness scoffs at *justice*,
—   Prov. 19:28a

To do righteousness and *justice*
is more acceptable to the Lord (יהוה Yahweh) than sacrifice.
—   Prov. 21:3

The violence of the wicked ensnares them
because they refuse to do what is *just*.
—   Prov. 21:7

When *justice* is done, it is a joy to the righteous
but dismay to the workers of evil.
—   Prov. 21:15

To respect faces (show partiality) in *judgment* is not good.
—   Prov. 24:23

Evil men (אִישׁ ish) do not understand justice,
but those seeking the Lord understand all.
— Prov. 28:5

A king by *judgment* establishes a land,
but a man (אִישׁ ish) taking bribes tears it down.
— Prov. 29:4

Many are seeking the face of a ruler,
but from the Lord (יהוה Yahweh) is *justice* for a man (אִישׁ ish).
— Prov. 29:26

 also:
A person (אָדָם adam) with the blood of a soul shall flee to the pit;
do not let them help him.
— Prov. 28:17

To show partiality is not good;
but for a piece of bread a virile man (גֶּבֶר gabor) will transgress.
— Prov. 28:21

injustice עַוְלָה ('awlah) (modern: injustice)

Speaking of David, the psalmist says, "An enemy exacts not upon him, and a son of injustice afflicts him not," 89:22. The word is very similar to the Hebrew word for burnt-offering, of which there are many more instances in the Hebrew Bible.

He who sows injustice will reap evil,
and the rod of his wrath will faith.
— Prov. 22:8

Knowledge דַּעַת (da'at) (modern: knowledge, mind)

Solomon prayed that all the peoples of the earth would know that the Lord is God, I Kings 8:60.

The fear of the Lord (יהוה Yahweh) is the beginning of
knowledge;
fools despise wisdom and discipline.
—   Prov. 1:7

How long will ... fools hate *knowledge*?
—   Prov. 1:22b

Because they hate *knowledge*
and did not choose the fear of the Lord (יהוה Yahweh),
would have none of my counsel,
and despised all of my correction,
therefore they shall eat the fruit of their way
and be sated with their own devoices.
—   Prov. 1:29-31

then you will know the fear of the Lord (יהוה Yahweh)
and find the knowledge of God (אֱלֹהִים Elohim).
For the Lord (יהוה Yahweh) gives wisdom
from His mouth come *knowledge* and understanding.
—   Prov. 2:5-6

for wisdom will come into your heart
and *knowledge* will be pleasant to your soul.
—   Prov. 2:10

By His *knowledge* the depths were broken up
and clouds drop dew.
—   Prov. 3:20

To observe thoughtfulness,
and *knowledge* do your lips keep.
—   Prov. 5:2

All the words of my mouth are
... right to those who find *knowledge*.

Take my ... *knowledge* rather than choice gold.
—   Prov. 8:8a, 9b, 10b

and *knowledge* of the Holy Ones is insight.
—   Prov. 9:10

The wise store up *knowledge,*
—   Prov. 10:14a

by *knowledge* the righteous are delivered.
—   Prov. 11:9

Whoever loves discipline loves *knowledge*,
—   Prov. 12:1a

A shrewd person conceals his *knowledge*,
—   Prov. 12:23a

Every shrewd one deals with *knowledge*,
—   Prov. 13:16a

but *knowledge* is easy for the one of understanding.
—   Prov. 14:6b

Leave the presence of a fool,
for there you do not meet words of *knowledge*.
—   Prov. 14:7

but the shrewd are crowned with *knowledge*.
—   Prov. 14:18b

The tongue of the wise makes *knowledge* good,
—   Prov. 15:2a

The lips of the wise scatter *knowledge*;
not so the minds of fools.
—   Prov. 15:7

The mind of him who has understanding seeks *knowledge,*
—   Prov. 15:14a

He who restrains his words has *knowledge,*
and he who has a cool spirit is a man (אִישׁ ish) of understanding.
—   Prov. 17:27

The heart of the prudent gets *knowledge,*
and the ear of the wise seeks *knowledge.*
—   Prov. 18:15

It is not good for a soul to be without *knowledge,*
—   Prov. 19:2a

and correct one with understanding, he will understand *knowledge.*
—   Prov. 19:25b

Cease, my son, to hear discipline
only to stray from words of *knowledge.*
—   Prov. 19:27

There is gold, and abundance of costly stones,
but the lips of *knowledge* are a precious jewel.
—   Prov. 20:15

When the scoffer is punished, the simple becomes wise,
and when the wise is instructed, he gains *knowledge.*
—   Prov. 21:11

The eyes of the Lord (יְהוָה Yahweh) keep watch over *knowledge,*
but he overthrows the words of the deceitful.
—   Prov. 22:12

Incline your ear, and hear the words of the wise,
and apply your mind to my *knowledge;*
for it will be pleasant if you keep them within you,
if all of them are ready on your lips.

That your trust may be in the Lord (יהוה Yahweh),
I have made them known to you today, even to you.
Have I not written for you 30 sayings of admonition and *knowledge*,
to show you what is right and true,
that you may return words of truth to those who sent you?
— Prov. 22:17-21

Bring in (i.e., apply) your mind to discipline
and your ear to words of *knowledge*.
— Prov. 23:12

By wisdom a house is built,
and by understanding it is established;
by *knowledge* the rooms are filled with all riches precious and pleasant.
A wise virile man (or warrior) (גֶּבֶר gbr) is strong,
a man (אִישׁ ish) of knowledge firms up strength;
for by wise guidance you can wage your war,
and in abundance of counselors there is victory.
Wisdom is too high for a fool;
in the gate he does not open mouth.
— Prov. 24:3-7

So *knowledge* of wisdom shall be to your soul;
when you find there is a future,
and your hope is not to be cut off.
— Prov. 24:14

(From King Hezekiah's scribes)
When a land transgresses it has many rulers;
but by a discerning person who *knows*, it is prolonged.
— Prov. 28:2

a wicked one does not discern *knowledge*.
— Prov. 29:7b

(From Agur of Massa)
Surely I am more brutish than any man (אִישׁ ish)
and am not a person (אָדָם adam) of understanding.
I have not learned wisdom and I do not have the *knowledge* of holiness.
—   Prov. 30:2-3

Law תּוֹרָה (torah) (modern: doctrine, teaching, law, Pentateuch, Torah)

English versions frequently translated this as a "mother's teaching," Prov. 1:8, but this translation does not communicate the full force of what the word "law" implies. The word is the same as the title of the first five books of the Hebrew Bible.

Heed, my son, your father's discipline
and do not forsake your mother's *law*
for they are an ornament of grace for your head
and necklaces for your neck.
—   Prov. 1:8-9

My son, do not forget my *laws*,
but let your heart keep my commandments;
for length of days and years of life and peace will they give you.
—   Prov. 3:1-2

For good teaching I give you:
My *law* do nor forsake.
—   Prov. 4:2

My son, keep your father's commandment,
and forsake not your mother's *law*.
Bind them upon your heart always;
tie them about your neck.
When you walk, they will lead you;
when you lie down, they will watch over you;
and when you awake, they will talk with you.

For the commandment is a lamp and the teaching a light,
and the corrections of discipline are the way of life,
to preserve you from the evil woman,
from the smooth tongue of the adventuress.
—   Prov. 6:20-24

My ... keep my *laws* as the apple of your eyes.
—   Prov. 7:2

The *law* of the wise is a fountain of life,
to avoid the snares of death.
—   Prov. 13:14

(From King Hezekiah's scribes)
Those who forsake the *law* praise the wicked,
but those who keep the *law* strive against them.
—   Prov. 28:4

He who keeps the *law* is a wise son
but the friend of gluttons shames his father.
—   Prov. 28:7

If one turns away his ear from hearing the *law*,
even his prayer is an abomination.
—   Prov. 28:9

Where there is no vision the people are let loose (RSV: cast off restraint).
but the keeper of the *law* is blessed.
—   Prov. 29:18

(From King Lemuel of Massa)
Her mouth she (a good wife) opens in wisdom
and the *law* of kindness is on her tongue.
—   Prov. 31:26

Mercy חֶסֶד (hesed) (modern: favor, charity, benevolence)

*Throughout the Hebrew Bible, mercy and truth are frequently
linked. The English versions frequently translate this combination
"loyalty and faithfulness," or, mercy as "loving kindness." None
capture the power of the notion of mercy. Naomi praised the
Lord's mercy, Ruth 2:20, and Rebecca praised Abaham's mercy
toward his master, Gen. 24:27.*

Mercy and truth you will not forsake;
bind them about your neck,
write them on the tablet of your heart.
So you will find favor and good repute in the sight of God and
person.
—   Prov. 3:3-4

A *merciful* man (אִישׁ ish) does well to his soul (i.e. benefits
himself),
—   Prov. 11:17a

but truth and *mercy* follow the devisers of good.
—   Prov. 14:22b

Righteousness exalteth a nation,
and the *mercy* of peoples is a sin-offering.
—   Prov. 14:34

By *mercy* and truth evil is covered,
—   Prov. 16:6a

The desire of a person (אָדָם adam) is *mercy*,
and it is better to be a poor man than a man (אִישׁ ish) of a lie.
—   Prov. 19:22

Many persons (אָדָם adam) will each proclaim his own *mercy*,
but who can find a truthful man (אִישׁ ish)?
—   Prov. 20:6

Mercy and truth preserve the king,
and his throne is upheld by *mercy*.
—   Prov. 20:28

He who pursues righteousness and *mercy*
finds life, righteousness and honor.
—   Prov. 21:21

(From King Lemuel of Massa)
She (a good wife) opens her mouth with wisdom,
and the teaching of *mercy* is on her tongue.
—   Prov. 31:26

Name, reputation שֵׁם (shem) (modern: name, title, fame)

The *name* of the Lord (יהוה Yahweh) is strong tower,
—   Prov. 18:10a

A good *name* is to be chosen rather than great riches,
 and grace better than silver or gold.
—   Prov. 22:1

 (From Agur of Massa)
Two things I ask of thee;
deny them not to me before I die:
Vanity and the word of a lie remove far from me
poverty and riches do not give to me,
lest I be full and deny thee
and say, "Who is the Lord (יהוה Yahweh)?"
or lest I be poor, and steal,
and profane the *name* of my God (אֱלֹהִים Elohim).
—   Prov. 30:7-9

Peace שָׁלוֹם (shalom) (modern: complete, full, entire, as well as a greeting and a farewell)

Peace is more than the absence of war; it is the fullness of life.

My son, do not forget my law,
but my commandments let your heart guard;
for length of days and years of life and *peace* will they give you.
—   Prov. 3:1-2

Her (wisdom's) ways are ways of pleasantness
and all her paths are *peace*.
—   Prov. 3:17

but to the counselors of *peace* is joy.
—   Prov. 12:20

When a man's (אִישׁ ish) ways please the Lord (יהוה Yahweh),
He makes even his enemies to be at *peace* with him.
—   Prov. 16:7

Rebuke, scold גְּעָרָה (ge'arah) (modern: rebuke, reproach)

Another word that is morally neutral, and not necessarily bad. "At thy rebuke, O God of Jacob, both rider and horse lay stunned," Psalms 76:7.

a scoffer does not hear a *rebuke*.
—   Prov. 13:1

the poor does not hear a *rebuke*.
—   Prov. 13:8

A *rebuke* goes into a discerning one
more than 100 blows into a fool.
—   Prov. 17:10

Truth and lies

The following verses contrast truth and lies.

He who speaks the truth reveals righteousness,
but a witness of falsehoods utters deceit
....
Lips of truth endure forever,
but a false tongue is but for a wink.
—   Prov. 12:17, 19

An abomination to the Lord (יהוה Yahweh) are lips of falsehood,
but those which do truth are His delight.
—   Prov. 12:22

A truthful witness does not lie,
but a false witness breathes out deceit.
—   Prov. 14:5

A truthful witness delivers souls,
but a deceitful one utters lies.
—   Prov. 14:25

truth אֱמֶת (`emeth)

Notice how frequently truth is linked to mercy and/or
righteousness. Occasionally English translations have defined as
אֱמֶת *(emeth) faithfulness. Note the following example, and how*
the power of the verse is enhanced when "steadfast love and
faithfulness" are retranslated as "mercy and truth."

Mercy and *truth* you will not forsake;
bind them about your neck,
write them on the tablet of your heart.
So you will find favor and good repute
in the sign of God (אֱלֹהִים Elohim) and a person (אָדָם adam)
—   Prov. 3:3-4

For *truth* my mouth will utter.
—   Prov. 8:7a (wisdom speaking)

The lip of *truth* is established for ever,
  and for a moment — a tongue of falsehood.
—   Prov. 12:19

but mercy and *truth* follow the devisers of good.
—   Prov. 14:22b

By mercy and *truth* evil is covered,
—   Prov. 16:6a

Many persons (אָדָם adam) will each proclaim his own mercy,
but who can find a *truthful* man (אִישׁ ish)?
—   Prov. 20:6

Mercy and *truth* preserve the king,
—   Prov. 20:28

Have I not written for you 30 sayings of admonition and
knowledge,
to show you what is right and *true*,
that you may return words of *truth* to him who sent you?
—   Prov. 22:20-21

Buy *truth*, and do not sell it;
buy wisdom, discipline, and understanding.
—   Prov. 23:23

A king who judges the poor with *truth*
his throne shall be established forever.
—   Prov. 29:14

   falsehood and lying

*Two Hebrew words mean lie, deceive, and act falsely: (שֶׁקֶר
(sheqer) and כָּזָב (kazar). We arbitrarily will define שָׁקַר
(shakar) as false and כָּזַב (kazav) as lying, the general usage of
English translations.*

The following verses use both words:

These six hath Jehovah hated, Yea, seven are abominations to His soul. Haughty eyes, a *false* tongue, and hands that shed innocent blood, a heart that devises wicked plans, feet that make haste to run to evil, a *false* witness who breathes out *lies*, and one who sows discord among brothers.
— Prov. 6:16-19

A faithful witness does not *lie*,
but a *false* witness breathes out *lies*.
— Prov. 14:5

A witness of *falsehoods* shall not be clean
and a breather of *lies* shall not escape.
— Prov. 19:5

false שֶׁקֶר (sheqer*)* (modern: lie, swindle, cheat*.)*

This is the word used in the Ninth Commandment, "You shall not bear false witness against your neighbor," Ex. 20:16.

He who conceals hatred has lips of *falsehood*,
and one sending out slander is a dullard.
— Prov. 10:18

The wicked is getting a *false* wage,
And whoso is sowing righteousness — a true reward.
— Prov. 11:18

but a *false* witness utters deceit.
— Prov. 12:17

The lip of truth is established for ever,
and for a moment — a tongue of *falsehood*.
— Prov. 12:19

A word of *falsehood*, the righteous hates,
— Prov. 13:5a

An evil doer is attentive to lips of vanity,
falsehood is giving ear to a mischievous tongue.
— Prov. 17:4

Not comely for a fool is a lip of excellency,
much less for a noble a lip of *falsehood*.
— Prov. 17:7

A witness of *falsehoods* will not go unpunished,
and a breather of deceit shall perish.
— Prov. 19:9

Bread of *falsehood* is sweet to a man (אִישׁ ish),
but afterward his mouth will be full of gravel.
— Prov. 20:17

The getting of treasures by a *false* tongue
is a fleeting vapor and a snare of death.
— Prov. 21:6

(From King Hezekiah's scribes)
Clouds and wind, and rain there is none,
(is) a man (אִישׁ ish) boasting himself of a *false* gift.
— Prov. 25:14

A man (אִישׁ ish) who bears *false* witness against his neighbor
is like a war club, or a sword, or a sharp arrow.
— Prov. 25:18

A *false* tongue hates those it crushes,
and a flattering mouth works ruin.
— Prov. 26:28

A ruler who is attending to false words,
all his ministers *are* wicked.
— Prov. 29:12

(From King Lemuel of Massa)
The grace is *false*, and the beauty *is* vain,
(but) a woman fearing the Lord (יהוה Yahweh), she may boast
herself.
— Prov. 31:30

lying כָּזָב (kazav) (modern: lie, deceive)

Delilah accused Samson of lying to her, Judges 16:10.

The desirability of a person (אָדָם adam) is his mercy
and it is better to be a poor man than a man (אִישׁ ish) of a *lie*.
— Prov. 19:22b

A *lying* witness will perish,
but a man (אִישׁ ish) that attends will speak forever.
— Prov. 21:28

Have no desire to his dainties, seeing it is *lying* food.
— Prov. 23:3

(From Agur of Massa)
Two things I ask of thee;
deny them not to me before I die:
Vanity and the word of a *lie* remove far from me
poverty and riches do not give to me,
lest I be full and deny thee
and say, "Who is the Lord(יהוה Yahweh)?"
or lest I be poor, and steal,
and profane the name of my God (אֱלֹהִים Elohim).
— Prov. 30:7-9

also:
Be not a witness against your neighbor without cause,
and do not deceive with your lips.
Do not say, "I will do to him as he has done to me;
I will pay the man (אִישׁ ish) for what he has done."
—   Prov. 24:28-29

(From King Hezekiah's scribes)
One who hates dissembles with his lips,
and in his inner being he lays up deceit.
—   Prov. 26:24

Wisdom חָכְמָה (shakhmah) (modern: wisdom)

The fear of the Lord is the beginning of knowledge;
fools despise *wisdom* and instruction.
—   Prov. 1:7

Wisdom cries aloud in the street;
in the markets she raises her voice; on top of the walls she cries
out;
at the entrance of the city gates she speaks:
"How long, O simple ones, will you love being simple?
How long will scoffers delight in their scoffing and fools hate
knowledge?
Give heed to my reproof;
behold, I will pour out my thoughts to you;
I will make my words known to you;
Because I have called and you refused to listen,
have stretched out my hand and no one has heeded,
and you have ignored all my counsel and would have none of my
reproof,
I also will laugh at your calamity;
I will mock when panic strikes you,
when panic strikes you like a storm,
and your calamity comes like a whirlwind,

when distress and anguish come upon you.
Then they will call upon me, but I will not answer;
they will seek me diligently but will not find me.
Because they hated knowledge and did not choose the fear of the
Lord (יהוה Yahweh),
would have none of my counsel,
and despised all my reproof,
therefore they shall eat the fruit of their way
and be sated with their own devices.
For the simple are killed by their turning away,
and the complacence of fools destroys them;
but he who listens to me will dwell secure
and will be at ease, without dread of evil.
—   Prov. 1:20-33

My son, if you receive my words
and treasure up my commandments with you,
making your ear attentive to *wisdom*
and inclining your heart to understanding;
yes, if you cry out for insight
and raise your voice for understanding,
if you seek it like silver and search for it as hidden treasures;
then you will understand the fear of the Lord (יהוה Yahweh)
and find the knowledge of God (אֱלֹהִים Elohim).
For the Lord (יהוה Yahweh) gives wisdom;
and from his mouth comes knowledge and understanding;
he stores up sound *wisdom* for the upright;
he is a shield to those who walk in integrity,
guarding the paths of justice and preserving the way of his saints.
Then you will understand righteousness and justice and equity,
every good path;
for *wisdom* will come into your heart,
and knowledge will be pleasant to your soul;
discretion will watch over you;
understanding will guard you;
delivering you from the way of evil,
from men (אִישׁ ish) of perverted speech,

who forsake the paths of uprightness to walk in the ways of
darkness,
who rejoice in doing evil and delight in the perverseness of evil;
whose paths are crooked,
and who are devious in their ways.
—   Prov. 2:1-15

Be not wise in your own eyes;
fear the Lord (היה Yahweh) and turn away from evil.
It will be healing to your navel and refreshment to your bones.
—   Prov. 3:7-8

Happy is the person (אדם adam) who finds wisdom,
and the person (אדם adam) who gets understanding,
for the gain from it is better than gain from silver
and its profit better than gold.
She is more precious than jewels,
and nothing you desire can compare with her.
Long life is in her right hand;
in her left hand are riches and honor.
Her ways are ways of pleasantness,
and all her paths are peace.
She is a tree of life to those who lay hold of her;
those who hold her fast are called happy.
The Lord (היה Yahweh) by *wisdom* founded the earth;
by understanding he established the heavens;
by his knowledge the deeps broke forth,
and the clouds drop down the dew.
My son, keep sound wisdom and discretion;
let them not escape from your sight,
and they will be life for your soul and adornment for your neck.
Then you will walk on your way securely and your foot will not
stumble.
If you sit down, you will not be afraid;
when you lie down you sleep will be sweet.
Do not afraid of sudden panic or of the ruin of the wicked, when it
comes;

for the Lord (יהוה Yahweh) will be your confidence and will keep
your foot from being caught.
— Prov. 3:13-26

The *wise* will inherit honor,
but fools get shame.
— Prov. 3:35

When I was a son with my father, tender,
the only one in the sight of my mother,
he taught me, and said to me,
"Let your heart hold fast my words,
and keep my commandments, and live;
do not forget, and do not turn away from the words of my mouth.
Get *wisdom*, get understanding.
Do not forsake her, and she will keep you;
love her, and she will guard you.
The beginning of *wisdom* is this:
Get *wisdom*, and whatever you get, get understanding.
Prize her highly, and she will exalt you;
she will honor you if you embrace her;
she will bestow on you a beautiful crown."
— Prov. 4:1-9

I have taught you the way of *wisdom*;
I have led you in the paths of uprightness.
— Prov. 4:10-11

My son, be attentive to my *wisdom*,
incline your ear to my understanding;
that you may keep discretion,
and your lips may guard knowledge.
— Prov. 5:1-2

Say to *wisdom*, "You are my sister,"
and call understanding your intimate friend.
— Prov. 7:4

Does not *wisdom* call?
Does not understanding raise her voice?
On the heights beside the way,
in the paths she takes her stand;
beside the gates in front of the town,
at the entrance of the portals she cries aloud:
"To you, O men (אִישׁ ish), I call,
and my cry is to the sons of persons (אָדָם adam).
O simple one, learn prudence;
O foolish ones, pay attention.
Hear, for I will speak noble things,
and from my lips will come what is right;
for my mouth will utter truth;
wickedness is an abomination to my lips.
All the words of my mouth are righteous;
there is nothing twisted or crooked in them.
They are all straight to him who understands
and right to those who find knowledge.
Take my instruction instead of silver,
and knowledge rather than choice gold;
for *wisdom* is better than jewels,
and all that you may desire cannot compare with her.
—   Prov. 8:1-11

I, *wisdom*, dwell in prudence,
and I find knowledge and discretion.
The fear of the Lord (יְהוָה Yahweh) is hatred of evil.
Pride and arrogance and the way of evil and perverted speech I
hate.
I have counsel and sound wisdom,
I have understanding, I have strength.
By me kings reign,
and rulers decree what is righteous;
by me princes rule,
and nobles govern the earth.
I love those who love me,
and those who seek me diligently find me.

I walk in the way of righteousness,
in the paths of justice,
endowing with substance those who love me,
and filling their treasuries.
The Lord (היה Yahweh) created me at the beginning of his work,
the first of his acts of old.
Ages ago I was set up,
at the first, before the beginning of the earth.
When there were no depths I was brought forth,
when there were no springs abounding with water.
Before the mountains had been shaped,
before the hills, I was brought forth;
before he had made the earth with its fields,
or the first of the dust of the world.
When he established the heavens, I was there,
when he drew a circle on the face of the deep,
when he made firm the skies above,
when he established the fountains of the deep,
when he assigned to the sea its limit,
so that the waters might not transgress his command,
when he marked out the foundations of the earth,
then I was beside him, like a master workman;
and I was daily his delight,
rejoicing before him always,
rejoiceing in his inhabited world
and delighting in the sons of men.
And now, my sons, listen to me;
happy are those who keep my ways.
Hear instruction and be wise, and do not neglect it.
Happy is the man (אִישׁ ish) who listens to me,
watching daily at my gates, waiting beside my doors.
For he who finds me finds life and obtains favor from the Lord
(היה Yahweh);
but he who misses me injures himself;
all who hate me love death."
Wisdom has built her house, she has set up her seven pillars.
She has slaughtered her beasts, she has mixed her wine,

she has also set her table.
She has sent out her maids to call from the highest places in town,
"Whoever is simple, let him turn in here!"
To him who is without sense she says,
"Come, east of my bread and drink of the wine I have mixed.
Leave simpleness, and live,
and walk in the way of insight."
He who corrects a scoffer gets himself abuse,
and he who reproves a wicked man incurs injury.
Do not reprove a scoffer, or he will hate you;
reprove a *wise* one, and he will love you.
Give instruction to the *wise* one, and he will be still wiser;
teach a righteous man and he will increase in learning.
The fear of the Lord (יהוה Yahweh) is the beginning of wisdom,
and the knowledge of the Holy One is insight.
For by me your days will be multiplied,
and years will be added to your life.
If you are *wise*, you are *wise* for yourself;
if you scoff, you alone will bear it.
—   Prov. 8:12-9:12

The *wise* of heart will heed commandments,
—   Prov. 10:8a

On the lips of him who has understanding is found *wisdom*,
—   Prov. 10:11a

The *wise* store up knowledge,
—   Prov. 10:14a

but *wise* conduct is pleasure to a man (איש ish) of understanding.
—   Prov. 10:23b

The mouth of the righteous brings forth *wisdom*,
—   Prov. 10:31a

but with the humble is *wisdom*.

—   Prov. 11:2b

and the fool will be servant to the *wise*.
—   Prov. 11:29b

but one listening to counsel is *wise*.
—   Prov. 12:15b

but the tongue of the *wise* brings healing.
—   Prov. 12:18b

A *wise* son heeds his father's discipline,
—   Prov. 13:1

but with those who take advice is *wisdom*.
—   Prov. 13:10b

The law of the *wise* is a fountain of life,
to avoid the snares of death.
—   Prov. 13:14

He who walks with the *wise* shall be *wise*,
—   Prov. 13:20

Wise women build their house,
—   Prov. 14:1a

but the lips of the *wise* will preserve them.
—   Prov. 14:3b

A scoffer seeks *wisdom* in vain,
—   Prov. 14:6b

The *wisdom* of a shrewd one is to discern his way,
—   Prov. 14:8a

The *wise* fears and turns from evil,

— Prov. 14:16a

The crown of the *wise* is their riches,
— Prov. 14:24a

Wisdom abides in the heart of one with understanding,
but it is not known in the heart of fools.
— Prov. 14:33

a servant who deals *wisely* has the king's favor,
— Prov. 14:35a

The tongue of the *wise* makes knowledge good,
— Prov. 15:2a

(A scoffer) will not go to the *wise.*
— Prov. 15:12b

A *wise* son makes a glad father,
— Prov. 15:20a

The ear that hears the correction of life will abide in *wisdom.*
— Prov. 15:31

A king's fury is a messenger of death,
and a *wise* man (אִישׁ ish) will cover it.
— Prov. 16:14

To get *wisdom* is better than gold,
— Prov. 16:16a

The *wise* of heart is called one of understanding,
— Prov. 16:21a

The heart of the *wise* makes his mouth prudent,
and adds persuasiveness to his lips.
— Prov. 16:23a

Why is there a price in the hand of a fool to buy *wisdom,* and not a mind?
— Prov. 17:16

With the face of the discerning is *wisdom,*
but the eyes of a fool are on the ends of the earth.
— Prov. 17:24a

Even a fool who keeps silent is considered *wise,*
when he closes his lips, he is thought (to be) understanding.
— Prov. 17:28

and the ear of the *wise* seeks knowledge.
— Prov. 18:15b

Hear counsel and accept discipline that you may be *wise* in the end.
— Prov. 19:20

and whoever is led astray by it (wine) is not *wise.*
— Prov. 20:1b

A *wise* king winnows the wicked,
and drives the wheel over them.
— Prov. 20:26

When the scoffer is punished, the simple becomes *wise,*
and when the *wise* is instructed, he gains knowledge.
— Prov. 21:11

Preasure treasure and oil are in a *wise* one's dwelling,
but a foolish person (אָדָם adam) devours it.
— Prov. 21:20

A *wise* one scales the city of the might
and brings down the stronghold in which they trust.
— Prov. 21:22

There is no *wisdom*, no understanding, no counsel against the Lord
(יהוה Yahweh).
—   Prov. 21:30

My son, if your heart is *wise*, my heart too will be glad.
—   Prov. 23:15

Hear, my son, and be *wise*, and direct your mind in the way.
—   Prov. 23:19

The father of the righteous will greatly rejoice;
he who begats a *wise* son will be glad in him.
Let your father and mother be glad,
let her who bore you rejoice.
—   Prov. 23:24-25

Buy truth, and do not sell it;
buy *wisdom*, instruction, and understanding.
—   Prov. 23:23

By *wisdom* a house is built, and by understanding it is established;
by knowledge the rooms are filled with all precious and pleasant
riches.
A *wise* virile man (or warrior) (גֶּבֶר gbr) is strengthened,
a man (אִישׁ ish) of knowledge firms up strength;
for by *wise* guidance you can wage your war,
and in abundance of counselors there is victory.
Wisdom is too high for a fool;
in the gate he does not open mouth.
—   Prov. 24:3-7

My son, eat honey, for it is good,
and the drippings of the honeycomb are sweet to your taste.
Know that *wisdom* is such to your soul;
if you find it, there will be a future, and your hope will not be cut
off.
          Prov. 24:13-14

(From King Hezekiah's scribes)
A rich man (אִישׁ ish) is *wise* in his own eyes,
but a poor one who has understanding will find him out.
—   Prov. 28:11

but he who walks in *wisdom* will be delivered.
—   Prov. 28:26

A man (אִישׁ ish) who loves *wisdom* makes his father glad,
a friend of whores wastes wealth.
—   Prov. 29:3

A fool brings out all of his spirit
the *wise* holding it back quiets it.
—   Prov. 29:11

The rod and reproof give *wisdom*
—   Prov. 29:13a

(From Agur of Massa)
Surely I am more brutish than any man (אִישׁ ish)
and am not a person (אָדָם adam) of understanding.
I have not learned *wisdom* and I do not have the knowledge of
holiness.
—   · Prov. 30:2-3

Four things on earth are small, but they are exceedingly *wise*:
the ants are a people not strong,
yet they provide their food in the summer;
the badgers are a people not mighty,
yet they make their homes in the rocks;
the locusts have no king,
yet all of them march in rank;
the lizard you can take in your hands,
yet it is in kings' palaces.
—   Prov. 30:24-28

(From King Lemuel of Massa)
She (a good wife) opens her mouth with *wisdom*,
and the teaching of mercy is on her tongue.
—   Prov. 31:26

Word דָּבָר (davar) (modern: say, speech, talk)

The importance of this word in Proverbs s how often it is attributed to Wisdom or God.

For understanding a proverb and its sweetness,\
words of the *wise* and their acute sayings.
—   Prov. 1:6

Turn back at my reproof, lo, I pour forth to you my spirit,
I make known my *words* with you.
—   Prov. 1:23 *(Wisdom is speaking)*

To deliverg you from the way of evil,
from ones of perverted *words.*
—   Prov. 2:12

(A father) taught me, and said to me,
"Let your heart hold fast my *words*; keep my commandments, and live;
—   Prov. 4:4

Hear, for I will *speak* noble things,
and from my lips will come what is right;
—   Prov. 8:6

In the abundance of *words* transgression ceases not,
and whoso is restraining his lips is wise.
—   Prov. 10:19

Sorrow in the heart of a man (אִישׁ ish) bows down,
and a good word makes him glad.

— Prov. 12:25

A false *word* the righteous hates,
— Prov. 13:5a

He who despises the *word* brings destruction on himself.
— Prov. 13:13a

In all labor there is advantage,
and a *word* of the lips is only to want.
— Prov. 14:23

A soft answer turneth back fury,
and a grievous *word* raiseth up anger.
— Prov. 15:1

To make an apt answer is a joy to a man (אִישׁ ish),
and a *word* in season, how good it is!
— Prov. 16:13

He who gives heed to the *word* will prosper,
and happy is he who trusts in the Lord (יהוה Yahweh).
— Prov. 16:20

And whoso is repeating a *word* is separating a familiar friend.
— Prov. 17:9

The *words* of a man's (אִישׁ ish) mouth are deep waters;
— Prov. 18:4a

The *words* of a tale-bearer are as self-inflicted wounds,
and they have gone down *to* the inner parts of the heart.
— Prov. 18:8

Whoso answers a *word*r before he hears,
 Folly it is to him and shame.
— Prov. 18:13

A false witness will perish,
but the *word* of a man (אִישׁ ish) who hears will endure.
—   Prov. 21:28

The eyes of the Lord (יהוה Yahweh) have kept knowledge,
and He overthrows the *words* of the treacherous.
—   Prov. 22:12

You will vomit up the morsels which you have eaten,
and waste your pleasant *words*.
—   Prov. 23:8

For destruction does their heart meditate,
and perverseness do their lips *speak*.
—   Prov. 24:2

Lips he kisses who returns straightforward *words*
—   Prov. 24:26.

(From King Hezekiah's scribes)
Apples of gold in imagery of silver,
is the *word* spoken at its fit times.
—   Prov. 25:11

He is cutting off feet, he is drinking injury,
who sends *words* by the hand of a fool.
—   Prov. 26:6
Be wise, my son, and rejoice my heart.
And I return my reproacher a *word*.
—   Prov. 27:11

A ruler who is attending to lying *words,*
all his ministers *are* wicked.
—   Prov. 29:12

You have seen a man hasty in his *words*!
More hope of a fool than of him.

—   Prov. 29:20

(From Agur of Massa)
The *words* of Agur son of Jakeh of Massa
—   Prov. 30:1a

Every *word* of God is tested;
he is a shield to those who take refuge in him.
Do not add to his words,
lest he rebuke you, and you be found a liar.
—   Prov. 30:5-6

(From King Lemuel of Massa)
The words of Lemuel, king of Massa, which his mother taught him:
—   Prov. 31:1a

INDEX

The Book of The Proverbs

Printed in the United States
1428900002B/196-213